CONTENTS

Contents

ABBREVIATIONS

FFHS	Federation of Family History Societies
FRC	Family Records Centre
GRO	General Register Office
HMC	Historical Manuscripts Commission
IGI	*International Genealogical Index*
LDS	Church of Jesus Christ of Latter-day Saints
NRA	National Register of Archives
OS	Ordnance Survey
PCC	Prerogative Court of Canterbury
PCY	Prerogative Court of York
PRO	Public Record Office
SoG	Society of Genealogists

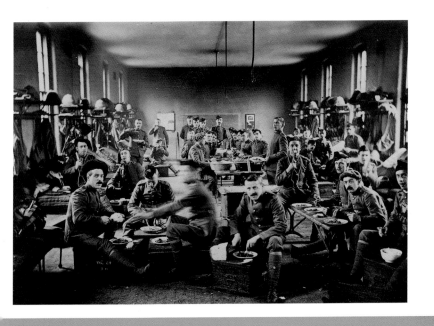

INTRODUCTION

Family history – genealogy – is one of the fastest-growing hobbies in Britain. Over the past 30 years tracking down ancestors has become an enormously popular pastime – perhaps a million people in Britain are engaged in the search. Genealogy has become the third most popular subject on the internet. You can be any age, creed, shape or size to start tracing your ancestors. All you need to get started is an enquiring mind, plus a notebook and sharp pencil. Why the pencil? Read on, and you'll find out.

Members of the North West Kent Family History Society at the The Church of St John the Baptist, West Wickham, 1999

Family history is something that you can pick up or put down when it suits you. After all, your ancestors are not going to disappear. How you tackle your research is up to you. There is no pressure to trace everyone you are descended from. Indeed, as you will discover, it is almost impossible to tick them all off. Most people end up only researching one side of their family or a few ancestors who particularly interest them. Others abandon their research at the beginning of the 19th century, which is about when the records become more difficult to use.

You'll find that there are enough challenges and puzzles to make tracing your ancestors stimulating. There's nothing quite like the buzz you get when you finally succeed in tracing that elusive great-grandmother! And if one of your forebears seems to appear from nowhere only to disappear irritatingly into the ether a few years later – well, there are plenty of other ancestors out there to track down.

THE FAMILY HISTORY SOCIETY OF CHESHIRE

THE WEB SITE FOR CHESHIRE GENEALOGY

Winner of the FFHS Site of the Year Award 2001

Registered Charity No. 515168

About the Society
Find out more about who we are and what we do.

How to Join
Print out our membership form, or join on-line using GENFAIR.

Research Centre
Members of the Society can make use of our extensive collection of reference materials at our Alderley Edge research centre.

Publications
A complete listing of all our book and microfiche publications, including the new Cheshire Marriage Indexes on CD-ROM

Research Advice
Although we don't do research for people, we can do our best to answer questions about researching in Cheshire.

Noticeboard
Latest news and events

E-mail
info@fhsc.org.uk

✦ ✦ ✦

Chairman
Mrs Brenda Smith
11 Thornway, High Lane, Stockport, Cheshire, SK6 8EL

Hon. Secretary
Mrs Hilda Massey,
101 Irby Road, Heswall,
Wirral, CH61 6UZ

✦ ✦ ✦

*We are a member of
The Federation of
Family History Societies*

CHESHIRE-L
The Cheshire Family History discussion group

Cheshire Surnames Directory
Register the names you are interested in, and find out if anyone else is tracing the same Cheshire families.

Cheshire BMD
Register Office indexes of births, marriages and deaths in the county.

Cheshire Towns and Parishes
The essential research information for each of the county's 500+ parishes and townships.

Cheshire Wills
A complete listing of over 70,000 wills preserved in the Cheshire Record Office, dating from 1492 to 1857.

Cheshire Genealogy
The GENUKI county page.

Links
Links to related sites.

One of the great things about this pastime is how friendly and helpful most family historians are. If you become confused on your first visit to the Family Records Centre (see p. 17), the chances are that someone at a neighbouring microfilm reader will be only too pleased to point you in the right direction. Genealogists are very sociable, as you will discover if you join a local family history society or a beginners' course at an adult education centre.

Family history can lead you in many new directions, including internet research

You may find that family history leads you into new and unexpected directions. One friend of mine has become the world expert on William Cuffey (the 19th-century black radical leader), while another has spent years tracing the ancestry of the Brontë sisters – who were rather more interesting than her own family!

What you do and how you do it is up to you – the only thing I ask is that you enjoy yourself.

Simon Fowler

Five generations of the Betts family, 1899 (COPY 1/440)

TEN FAMILY HISTORY COMMANDMENTS

1   Don't bite off too much at once. To begin with, limit yourself to one side of the family or an individual who interests you. Start by choosing someone you have some information about. If you are not sure who to choose, it is usually easier to research people with unusual surnames.

2   One of the problems you'll soon encounter is the mass of notes, certificates and photocopies you collect during your researches. So you need to create a system that will keep this information in a way that allows you to find it easily in future. If you have a computer, there are a number of software packages that store information and present it as family trees. A decent program costs about £50. A simple low-tech solution is to provide individual folders to keep information about each ancestor.

3   If you have a computer but are not already on the internet, it is well worth getting online. It needn't cost very much, and the resources available on the internet can really help your research. A list of useful websites is provided on p. 78.

4   While visiting record offices, obey the rules – particularly when handling original documents. They are a unique part of Britain's heritage. Once destroyed, they can't be replaced.

5   If you are using a register or other large volume, check to see whether there is an index at the front or back. If not and it contains lots of names, ask the staff whether volunteers have prepared an index.

6   If you are unsure of anything, ask the staff. They are there to help and are often very knowledgeable about the records and their quirks. Treat the staff with courtesy and they will normally be only too willing to impart this knowledge – perhaps saving you days of work.

War records for Cecil Charles Noble, World War I

7 Note down everything of interest in a notebook, including the reference of the relevant document or book. Try to make your notes legible. When you get home, transfer the information to your files or information-storage system as soon as possible.

8 Never trust the information you download from the internet or find in indexes to records. Mistakes are made, so you need to check everything against the original sources. Otherwise, you could waste a lot of time (maybe years!) trying to trace people who are not related to you.

9 It is common for the spelling of surnames to change over time; also, be alert to the possibility of variants and misspellings. There are a host of reasons for such variations, but the most important is that spelling was not fixed until the 18th century. In addition, bureaucrats often make mistakes when writing down names and their mistakes are perpetuated in the records.

10 Even if you have no ancestors from the area where you live, it is worth joining a local family history society. Societies publish newsletters and journals, and organize meetings where you can listen to experts and share experiences with fellow enthusiasts. Most run regular trips to the Public Record Office and Family Records Centre in London. Also, you can give something back by becoming involved in indexing or other projects that will be of help to other researchers.

STARTING AT HOME

When piecing together your family tree, start by thinking about what you know already. Obviously the more information you have to start with, the better – but if you know next to nothing, there's no need to panic.

The author's great aunt, Philippa Mary Crozier

Family history books often tell you to start by talking to the oldest members of the family – and that can be extremely fruitful. But many people do not develop an interest in where they come from until late in life, and you have to work with what you've got. An all too common lament is 'I wish I had asked Granny when she was still alive!'

Most families have a collection of heirlooms. These vary tremendously, but they are a good starting point and may tell you something about your immediate ancestors. If you can't find much in your own home, other members of the family may be able to help. And it's always worth asking around. My father recently produced a large envelope full of goodies, which contained papers and photographs about ancestors going back 150 years – although it is not clear at present who is linked to whom.

Further reading

Iain Swinnerton, *Sources for Family History in the Home* (FFHS, 1995)

The sort of things you might find are:

Family Register
template, 1898
(COPY 1/43(ii))

- Photographs and photograph albums (more about photographs in a minute).
- Letters and diaries. These can be poignant. I always regret that when my grandmother died, the last (unopened) letters from her favourite brother, killed in the last days of the First World War, were thrown away.
- Official papers – from birth and marriage certificates to National Identity Cards and call-up papers.
- Press cuttings about members of the family. My father's papers contain funeral notices for the Rev. George Paul Belcher and his wife who died in the 1880s – so presumably we are related in some way.
- Family bibles – which may have details of births, christenings, marriages and deaths inscribed in them. If you're very lucky, the information may go back centuries.
- Artefacts. Silver and portraits are often passed down and may be inscribed. Wedding dresses and christening clothes are also commonly passed on from generation to generation.

Christmas card
from the author's
grandfather to his
grandmother

Looking after heirlooms

The PRO Conservation Department at work

You should seek professional advice, without delay, about items in poor condition. However, with a little care you can preserve documents and other heirlooms for future generations to enjoy. In particular, guard against the following perils:

Heat Being kept at too warm a temperature is particularly bad for paper, as it will dry out and become brittle.

Water Leaking pipes and damp rooms are a great threat to heirlooms. Paper is capable of absorbing large amounts of water in damp conditions. As a result, it is likely to buckle or the ink may run.

Light Strong light is a problem, as it causes fading. Direct sunlight is the most harmful form. Don't place valuable or treasured photographs and paintings on walls or mantelpieces where sunlight can get at them. Why not display reproductions instead?

Mould This is likely to form when items are left in damp conditions and can cause serious damage. If you find evidence of mould, seek professional advice.

Handling Old documents and photographs suffer from being handled, so why not get copies made and take these on your research trips? Pick up documents and photos by the edge to prevent passing potentially damaging grease from your fingers to the document or the surface of the photograph.

Your family heirlooms should be kept in a cool, dark, dry place. I keep my papers under the bed in my north-facing spare room. As added protection against light and damp, it is also advisable to store them in boxes with tight-fitting lids. Shoe boxes (provided they are large enough) will do, at least as a start. Ensure that individual documents and photographs will not get creased or folded – and don't be tempted to use sticky tape to mend damaged documents, as the tape will eventually become brittle and mark the document permanently.

Further reading

Leaflets on aspects of paper and photograph conservation are available from the Public Record Office. Also, family history magazines often include items on conservation, for example, 'Preserving Historic Documents at Home', in *Family History Monthly*, December 2000.

Old photographs can suffer from repeated handling. 2nd Army Corps staff officers, April 1903 (COPY 1/460)

Mainly for younger family historians!

You are the lucky ones, some of your ancestors are still alive! Interview them now, before it is too late to build up a picture of them and their lives. Ask them about:

Their parents and grandparents When and where they were born, got married and died. What did they do? And who were their relations?

Other members of the family Who they were and what happened to them.

Childhood What was it like growing up? What were their experiences at school?

Adulthood Getting married and raising a family, their experiences at work, and notable events in their lives such as the Second World War.

What you ask will, of course, depend on the individual you are talking to. It's often a good idea to rough out a list of questions before you start. This will help to give the interview focus and ensure you don't forget anything important.

When preparing for the interview, bear in mind that:

- Old people get tired easily – so don't try to cover too much ground at once.
- If you plan to use a tape recorder, before you start make sure the person you are talking to doesn't mind being recorded. Also, that the machine is working properly and you have spare batteries and tapes.
- You may find that the interviewee is unwilling to talk about a particular topic – perhaps the early death of a loved one or some shameful family scandal. Respect this desire for privacy by changing the subject.

Family photographs

Members of your family may well have a number of old photographs. These should be treasured, because they offer a real link to the past. You may find photographs of ancestors at various stages in their lives, as well as family groups, events such as weddings or christenings, and snapshots of areas in which family members lived – perhaps showing bomb damage or a royal visit.

The earliest photographs date from the 1840s, and almost immediately became immensely popular. Photographic studios where people could have portraits taken sprang up around the country. Slow exposure times meant that the sitter had to keep absolutely still, which is why most early pictures look so posed.

The 1890s saw the first commercially produced hand-held cameras, such as the Kodak Box Brownie, which were cheap enough to allow millions of people to take up the hobby. Picture postcards also became very popular. Although service personnel were not supposed to take cameras on active service during the two world wars, the rule was widely broken – so there are lots of pictures available, particularly for the Second World War. These are generally black-and-white, as it was only after the Second World War that colour film became commonly used.

Old photographs sometimes pose problems. For example, it can be difficult to work out who appears in the picture, and when and where it was taken. There are several ways to overcome such difficulties:

- Ask older relations whether they can help.
- Dress fashions may well suggest an approximate date. During the world wars there may be shots of family members in uniform – in which case,

The author's grandmother with nursing colleagues during the First World War

regimental buttons and cap badges should indicate which unit a serviceman was with.

- Documents such as birth and marriage certificates may provide a clue, if you know somebody was born or married at a certain time.
- Always look at the back of a photograph. There may be a handwritten note, and the name and address of the studio where the picture was taken may be printed on the back or on the mount. Local trade directories or a directory of well-known photographers and photographic studios may give an idea when a studio was in operation.
- You may be able to guess the approximate ages of people in a photo. However, before the Second World War people tended to age much earlier – so by today's standards even fairly young people can look old.

Further reading

There are a number of books about photographs and family history, including:

Robert Pols, *Family Photographs 1860–1945* (PRO, 2002)

Robert Pols, *Identifying Old Photographs* (FFHS, 1998)

Checklist to get you started

This checklist will help you make the most of the information you already have about your family's history. Don't worry if you know next to nothing – the purpose of this book is to help you find out more.

1. Have you looked for personal papers – such as letters, diaries and official documents?

2. Have you looked for family photographs?

3. Have you talked to elderly relations about their memories of the family?

4. Are there any interesting stories about your family and its history?

5. Do you know:
   - When and where your parents were born?
   - When and where they got married?
   - When they died and where they are buried?
   - What they did for a living?

6. Do you know:
   - When and where your four grandparents were born?
   - When and where they got married?
   - When they died and where they are buried?
   - What they did for a living?

7. Do you know:
   - When and where any of your eight great-grandparents were born?
   - When and where they got married?
   - When they died and where they are buried?
   - What they did for a living?

VISITING ARCHIVES

At some stage in our search you're going to need to visit record offices – also referred to as archives. You may be apprehensive about this; but don't worry, the natives are friendly and pretty helpful! In fact most people enjoy their time so much they can't wait to go back.

The PRO Microfilm Reading Room

Record offices differ from libraries in at least one important respect. Unlike libraries, where books on the same subject are grouped together, archival material is normally arranged by who gave the material rather than by subject. For example, at the Public Record Office all War Office records have the prefix WO; and at local record offices the records of a particular council or business are normally kept together. Another difference is that almost all the documents or files you will be looking at are unique, so users are asked to take great care in handling them. Even microfilm can be damaged and takes time to replace.

Before you visit an archive, telephone to check that they have the items you are looking for and, if necessary, to book a seat. After all, it's a waste of your time and may be a bit embarrassing to turn up at an archive only to find they're closed or haven't got room for you.

Take with you a notebook (apart from the likelihood of mislaying notes made on scraps of paper, loose sheets are prohibited in some archives) and a pencil or two – as pens are not allowed in record offices, because of the damage they can do to irreplaceable documents. You may also want to take a packed lunch with you, plus a £1 coin or two for lockers and some extra money in case you decide to have copies of documents made.

Family Records Centre

The FRC is a joint service run by the Office for National Statistics (ONS) and the Public Record Office. It is an essential port of call for family historians, holding indexes to many of the major sources for family history in England and Wales, including birth, marriage and death records. There are also microfilm copies of a wide range of documents including the census. In addition, there are an increasing number of online search facilities including from January 2002 the 1901 census and a link to the General Register Office for Scotland in Edinburgh, as well as a large collection of reference books, indexes and maps. No original documents, however, are kept at the FRC.

An exterior view of the FRC

You will need to visit the FRC to:

- Consult indexes to birth, marriage and death certificates from July 1837 (see pp. 22–4)
- Use census returns from 1841 to 1891 (see pp. 36–41)
- Use Prerogative Court of Canterbury wills (see pp. 42–5)
- Use nonconformist parish registers (see pp. 32–3)

The ground floor contains material relating to births, marriages and deaths; you can order copies of the certificates (see p. 24). Other records are on the first floor. In the basement are lockers, drinks machines and a place for you to eat your sandwiches. There is also a bookshop.

You don't need to make an appointment to visit the FRC. It is open Monday to Saturday (closed Sundays and bank holidays). The opening hours are:

Monday	9 a.m. to 5 p.m.
Tuesday	10 a.m. to 7 p.m.
Wednesday	9 a.m. to 5 p.m.
Thursday	9 a.m. to 7 p.m.
Friday	9 a.m. to 5 p.m.
Saturday	9.30 a.m. to 5 p.m.

Family Records Centre
1 Myddelton Street
London EC1R 1UW
General enquiries: 020 8392 5300
Birth, marriage, death and adoption
  enquiries: 0870 243 7788
Fax: 020 8392 5307
Internet: www.familyrecords.gov.uk

Public Record Office

The PRO is big, really big. When you arrive on your first visit, you may think you'll never find your way around it. But it's actually very simple, and there are lots of friendly and knowledgeable staff and simply written leaflets to help you find what you want.

You'll need to visit the PRO to see:

- Records for officers and other ranks who served in the Army and Navy up to the end of 1920 (see pp. 47–55)
- Records relating to railwaymen, emigrants and immigrants, some courts, the Metropolitan Police and some categories of civil servants (see pp. 64–73)
- Tithe, enclosure and valuation maps (see pp. 62–3)

You will not, however, find:

- Newspapers
- Many records relating to Scotland (most of these are in Edinburgh)
- Many records relating to Ireland (most of these are in Dublin and Belfast)
- Parish records (for these you will need to go to local record offices or the Society of Genealogists)
- Many records relating to businesses and organizations (for these you will need to go to local record offices)

The PRO entrance

There are five reading areas and enquiry points:

Research Enquiries Room Where you can use the computer catalogues, order documents, or discuss your research with the staff. Various indexes to the records and reference books are also to be found here.

Document Reading Room Where you can read the more modern original documents.

Map and Large Document Reading Room Situated on the top floor, this is where maps and other large documents can be viewed. In addition, if your interests lie in Tudor times or earlier periods, there are specialist staff here who can help you.

Microfilm Reading Room Where you will find the increasing number of records that can only be seen on microfilm. You do not need to order these documents, as the material is available in cabinets from which you help yourself. Records to be found here include some of the First World War service records (see p. 53).

Library Situated next door to the Microfilm Reading Room, the library has a wide range of books and journals of help to family historians, including the *Gentleman's Magazine*, and a selection of directories.

To use the PRO you will need a reader's ticket, which you can get on your first visit. To obtain one, you need to bring identification such as a banker's card or full driving licence or (if you are not a British citizen) your passport. You don't need an appointment and the opening times are similar to those of the FRC, although the PRO is normally closed for stocktaking during the first week of December.

The PRO has a car park, and there are lockers for your luggage. Its amenities include a restaurant, a well-stocked bookshop and a fascinating small museum, where the Domesday Book and a facsimile of Magna Carta are displayed.

Checking in at reception

Public Record Office
Kew
Richmond
Surrey TW9 4DU
Tel: 020 8876 3444 (general)
Enquiries and advance ordering of
   documents, with exact references
   only: 020 8392 5200
Internet: www.pro.gov.uk

Local record offices

Each county has its own record office, and so do some cities. Local studies libraries may also have material that can assist you.

The holdings of local archives vary greatly, but you are likely to find:

- Parish records – not only parish registers but accounts, magazines and other material, too (see pp. 28–35).
- Poor law records
- Records of quarter sessions and other local courts
- Records of local government, businesses (such as breweries, farms and mines), organizations such as charities, clubs and friendly societies, and personal papers deposited by individuals
- Local maps
- Local newspapers – and, at local studies libraries, indexes and cuttings
- Microfilm copies of censuses and other national records relating to the area

There is a nationwide index to this material at the National Register of Archives (NRA), which is part of the Historical Manuscripts Commission (HMC). Their database is online at www.hmc.gov.uk, or you can phone them on 020 7242 1198. Alternatively, you can write to them or visit the HMC. So it is a fairly easy task to find out who has what.

The HMC also maintains a database of archives, so can tell you which is your local archive and where it is. However, it may be easier to look in Yellow Pages. Details of libraries can be found at www.familia. org.uk; addresses, telephone numbers and URLs (website addresses) for record offices and libraries are included in the annual *Family and Local History Handbook* (also known as the *Genealogical Services Directory*).

Historical Manuscripts Commission

**Quality House
Quality Court
Chancery Lane
London WC2A 1HP**

Local planning map of Sheffield, Yorkshire (HLG 5/1859)

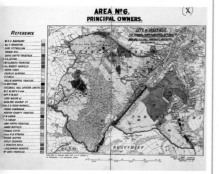

Five easy options

Microfilm and the internet have made it much easier to see records and consult indexes without having to travel very far or even, increasingly, without leaving your home.

1 **The internet** From January 2002 you will be able to see scanned images from the 1901 census online at www.census.pro.gov.uk, followed within a year by the 1881 and 1891 returns. In addition, a number of local record offices and the Society of Genealogists are putting catalogues and indexes on the internet. In some cases there is a charge for viewing indexes and images, although they normally work out cheaper than a trip to London.

2 **Family History Centres** The Mormons Church of Jesus Christ of Latter-day Saints (LDS) runs a network of family history centres that are open to everybody free of charge. They have filmed most of the important genealogical records, but may have to order certain reels from Salt Lake City for you. The LDS family history centres are listed in Yellow Pages and at www.lds.org.uk.

3 **The Society of Genealogists** The SoG has Britain's finest genealogical library, with over 100,000 volumes and copies of records on microfilm. They also have a large collection of family trees and personal research donated by family historians over many years. If you are not a member, using the library (which is open between Tuesday to Saturday from 10 a.m. to 6 p.m. and 8 p.m. Wednesdays and Thursdays) costs £3 per hour, £8 per half day or £12 per day. An increasing number of their indexes are available online, for a fee, at www.englishorigins.net.
Society of Genealogists
14 Charterhouse Buildings
Goswell Road
London
EC1M 7BA
Tel: 020 7251 8799
Internet: www.sog.org.uk

4 **Local record offices and local studies libraries** These often have copies of national records for their areas, plus various indexes, and many of them have computers that you can use for internet access.

5 **Local family history societies** These may well be able to help you track down ancestors in a particular district. Some of them will do simple research for you, but they are more likely to either recommend researchers who undertake the work for a fee or tell you which local archives can help you. Family history societies are listed at www.ffhs.org.uk, and your local library may have details of the ones in your area.

CIVIL REGISTRATION

How could you prove when and where you were born or got married, or indeed whether you are still alive? The answer would be to contact the General Register Office (see p. 24), which registers these vital events and issues legal certificates as proof. But although such a system may seem both straightforward and desirable, it was not until July 1837 that civil registration was set up for England and Wales.

Before then people had, by law, to be christened, married and buried by the Church of England. Parish registers acted, in theory, both as a form of national registration and as evidence that individuals were members of the established church. Until 1829 applicants for government positions, such as naval or army officers, had to prove that they were Anglicans. Consequently the PRO has several small collections of certificates issued by local vicars, and you may occasionally find copies elsewhere. By the 1830s, the old system had broken down. More and more nonconformists and Catholics chose their own churches to celebrate these events. Also, there were relatively few Anglican churches in the rapidly growing industrial areas of the North.

Baptism solemnised in the Parish Church of St. Peter, in Liverpool, in the County of Lancaster, in the Year One Thousand *eight* Hundred and *twenty three*

Anglican baptism certificate, 1823 (WO 42)

The system

Births, marriages and deaths are registered with 600 or so local registrars, who keep their own registers as well as sending details to the General Register Office for inclusion in the national register. Both the GRO and local registrars can issue certificates giving details of births, marriages and deaths.

Until 1875 it was not compulsory to register these events. It is thought that perhaps 15 per cent of births were not registered in some parts of England and Wales; in addition, a recent study has discovered mistakes in the marriage indexes.

Even after 1875, births, marriages and deaths could fail to be registered. For my own part, I've been unable to find the birth certificate for my grandfather, who was born in September 1894. If you find yourself in this position and know roughly where the event took place, there are three possible avenues of research. You can ask the local register office whether they are able to help, or search the local parish registers, or try to find your ancestor in the census returns.

The most important pieces of information you need before you can start is the approximate date and place where the event occurred. If you don't know this, then it helps if you are researching an unusual surname. Even an unusual forename may be of use (my grandfather was called Paul, which was fairly uncommon in the 1890s).

You will find indexes for the whole of England and Wales at the Family Records Centre. Microfiche copies are widely available at large libraries, LDS family history centres (see p. 21) and the Society of Genealogists. Some family history societies also have sets; and there is a project to put them onto the internet at http://freebmd.rootsweb.com/.

St Giles' Church, Cripplegate, City of London, 1815

Consulting the registers at the Family Records centre

General Register Office

PO Box 2
Southport
Merseyside PR8 2JD
Tel: 0870 243 7788
Email:
  certificate.services@ons.gov.uk
Internet:
  www.statistics.gov.uk/nsbase/
  registration/default.asp

You will need to use these indexes to find the relevant references so you can order certificates. There are four quarters per year: January to March, April to June, July to September, and October to December. Since people had six weeks to register the event, it is not uncommon, for example, to find the entry for a March birth in the April–June volume.

Early index volumes are handwritten and can be difficult to read. The more modern volumes are also slightly more informative than earlier ones. For instance, from 1866 the age of the deceased was added to the entries in death indexes; and in 1912 the names of both spouses were included in the marriage volumes.

Once you have the necessary information, you can then order certificates – either in person at the Family Records Centre (see p. 17), where a certificate will cost you £6.50, or by post or telephone at the General Register Office.

Ordering by post costs £8 if you already have the reference, and £11 if you don't. The GRO plans online ordering in the near future. Meanwhile, their website gives more information about the services they offer.

Alternatively you can obtain certificates from local register offices – but only for the area they are responsible for. Addresses of local registries are given in *The Family and Local History Handbook*, in Yellow Pages and at www.genuki.org.uk/big/eng/RegOffice/.

You might also try

Newspapers and magazines

Marriages and funerals often receive press coverage, with photographs and lists of people present. Unusual or tragic deaths were always a popular topic. Births, marriages and deaths are often announced in the small ads. *The Times* is the most famous place for notices of this sort, but virtually all local and national newspapers from the 1850s included them.

Company magazines and journals often record marriages of employees, the birth of their children, and the passing of former colleagues.

Parish magazines usually list christenings, marriages and burials. Their survival is patchy, but good places to try are the local studies library or record office.

Parish registers

Although obviously much less important than civil registration, parish registers (see pp. 28–31) continue to be kept after 1837 (as they are today). If you know which church the event took place in, the relevant register should be fairly easy to find. However, if you already have the certificate, the register probably won't provide any additional information.

Probate registers

Entries in the registers of wills at the Principal Probate Registry (see p. 43) contain almost as much information as can be found in the death certificate itself.

Further reading

David Annal, *Getting Started in Family History* (PRO, revised edition 2001)

David Annal, *Using Birth, Marriage, and Death Records* (PRO, revised edition 2001)

Tom Wood, *An Introduction to British Civil Registration* (FFHS, 2000)

Also, you might want to look at Barbara Dixon's introduction to civil registration from the point of view of a registrar on http://home.clara.net/dixons/Certificates/indexbd.htm

'There's no mistake in that'; music cover, c. 1860

What the certificates tell you

Birth, marriage and death certificates are the most important documents you will need for your research. Although the certificates are fairly expensive, they are a worthwhile investment – for they contain information you can't find elsewhere, such as the exact date and place of events, addresses, jobs and parents' names. To minimize the amount you spend, make sure you have as much information as possible before you order. There are lots of entries for people named John Smith born in London – but far fewer for Julius John Smith born in Fulham.

Marriage certificates
These give you the following information:
- Date and place of the marriage
- Full names of the bride and groom
- Ages of bride and groom
  (if an entry says 'of full age', that means 21 or over)
- Occupations of bride and groom
- Residence at time of marriage
  (if both parties give the same address they were not usually living together, but were trying to save the expense of having banns called in two parishes)
- Name and occupation of the father of the bride and the father of the groom
- Witnesses (most frequently friends or relations)

Death certificates
These include the following information:
- **Date and place of death**
- **Name of the deceased**
- **Age**
  (this may be approximate)
- **Occupation**
- **Cause of death**
  (this is often imprecise or given in medical jargon – but unusual circumstances, such as dying in a railway accident, may be described)
- **Informant**
  (usually a member of the family or the doctor)

Birth certificates
These give you the following items of information:

Date and place of birth
(if an exact time is given this usually indicates twins or a multiple birth)

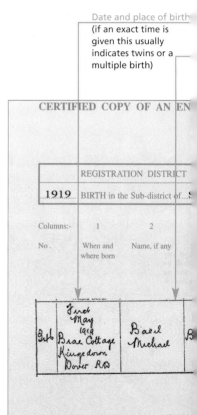

CERTIFIED COPY OF AN EN

REGISTRATION DISTRICT

...1919... BIRTH in the Sub-district of...S

Columns:-	1	2
No.	When and where born	Name, if any
Birth	First May 1919 Brae Cottage Kingsdown Dover RD	Basil Michael	B

CERTIFIED to be a true copy of an entry in

Given at the GENERAL REGISTER OFFIC

BXBZ 296929

Birth certificate
and photograph
of Basil Michael
Fowler

Father's name and occupation
(illegitimacy is shown by the
absence of a father's name)

Mother's name and maiden name
(the mother's maiden name can
help in searches for marriage
certificates)

ne and sex

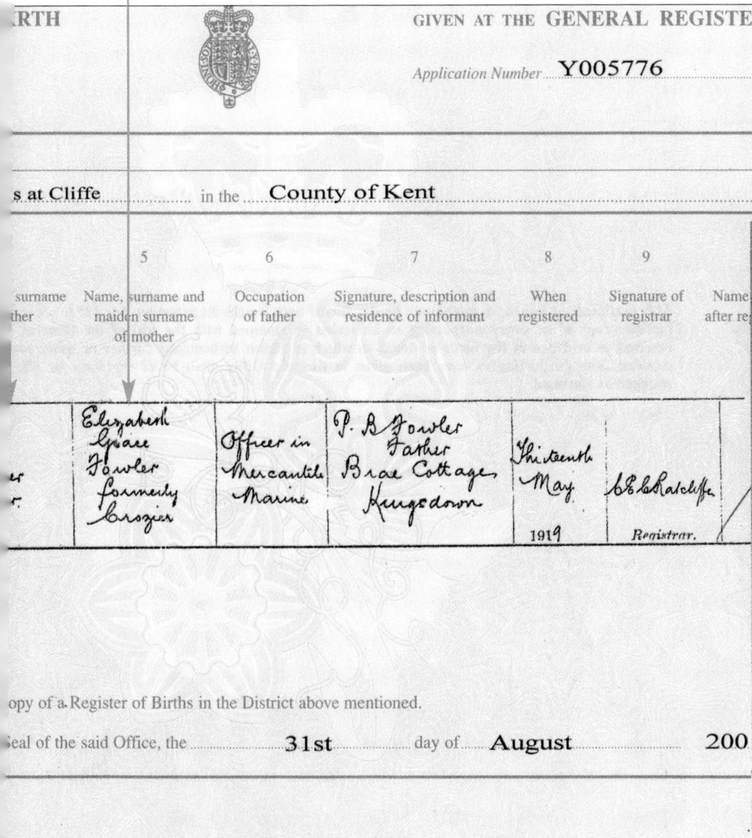

RTH

GIVEN AT THE **GENERAL REGISTER OFFICE**

Application Number **Y005776**

s at Cliffe in the **County of Kent**

	5	6	7	8	9	
surname ther	Name, surname and maiden surname of mother	Occupation of father	Signature, description and residence of informant	When registered	Signature of registrar	Name after re
	Elizabeth Grace Fowler formerly Crozier	Officer in Mercantile Marine	P. B Fowler Father Brae Cottage Kingsdown	Thirteenth May 1919	A.E.E.Ratcliffe Registrar.	

opy of a Register of Births in the District above mentioned.

Seal of the said Office, the **31st** day of **August** **200**

PARISH RECORDS

When you start to trace your ancestors back into the early 19th century, you'll increasingly have to rely on parish registers. The good news is that there are several nation-wide indexes – but the records were often poorly kept or just do not survive, which can be frustrating.

'Signing the marriage register' by Charles James, 1896

The Anglican Church, or Church of England, is by law the established church of England and, until 1920, Wales. Until 1837 it was compulsory for you to baptize your children, get married in church and be buried in hallowed ground. The Church was also responsible for proving wills (see p. 44) and had a role in running secular affairs in rural parishes.

There were, and indeed still are, some 16,000 parishes across England and Wales. Most villages were within a single parish, although towns had two or more parishes, depending on their size and on the wealth of benefactors in medieval times. Each parish elected two churchwardens to assist the incumbent vicar or rector, and in larger or wealthier districts appointed a clerk who was responsible for maintaining the registers and keeping parish records safe. If the clergy and their clerks were conscientious, then that is a great bonus for family historians. However, this was not always the case. In Richmond, Surrey, the same family held the post of clerk for generations – which, according to the transcriber of the records, resulted in 'a tradition of slovenliness and neglect in regard to their duty'. This meant that many baptisms, marriages and deaths were either not recorded or incompletely noted in the register, and thus are lost for ever.

Although the Church of England was the only legal church, there were of course other churches that engaged in worship. Roman Catholics, for example, did not entirely disappear with the Reformation in the 16th century. Despite terrible persecution, parts of south Lancashire remained loyal to the old religion – as did odd pockets elsewhere, especially where a local landowning family remained believers. But a bigger threat to the Church came from the newer denominations. These nonconformists, as they were known, began with the Quakers and Baptists in the mid 17th century. The most important sect, however, was the Methodists, who came to prominence in the 18th century. All this means that to find your ancestors you may need to check the records of other denominations as well as Anglican parish registers.

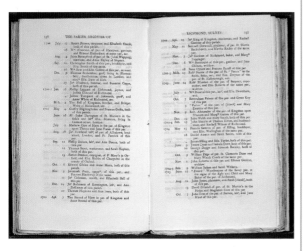

Transcript of a parish register, 1583–1720, for Richmond, Surrey

The Church of England

The Reverend Frank Swainson, 1903 (COPY 1/467)

Parish registers were first kept in 1538 and are, of course, maintained today. Few records survive before the beginning of the 17th century. The only major change since then was the introduction in 1813 of printed forms in which specified details are entered.

The survival of early registers is patchy, and they can be depressingly unhelpful. Baptismal entries often consist of little more than the child's name, who the father was, and when the event took place. Baptisms normally occurred within a few days of the birth. If the child was born out of wedlock, this would also be noted and the mother's name given. Before 1754, entries for weddings usually contain the names of the spouses, with perhaps a note if one of them was born outside the parish. After 1754, marriage entries had to be entered in special registers and are a little more informative. Death registers normally just contain the name of the deceased, although occasionally their age and occupation is noted.

Matters are made worse by the relatively small number of Christian names in general use. You may well find three or four babies with the same forename and surname christened within a few months of each other, making it impossible to work out from whom you are descended.

If the register you are looking for is missing, it is worth enquiring whether a bishop's transcript survives. Clerks had to make copies, as a matter of routine, and send them to the bishop for safekeeping. However, as they were not paid for this task, the quality of the transcript is often poor.

Most parish registers and bishops' transcripts are with local record offices. They are not with the PRO or FRC, and it is now rare for individual churches to keep their old registers. Cecil Humphrey-Smith, *The Phillimore Atlas and Index to Parish Registers* (Phillimore, 1995) will tell you where registers are held. Most archives and local libraries have copies.

A large number of registers have been transcribed. The largest collection of these transcripts is held by the Society of Genealogists. The Society also has Boyd's Marriage Index, which includes details of about one in eight of the marriages that took place between 1538 and 1837. This index is being put online at www.englishorigins.net, where it may be searched for a fee.

Also helpful are the *International Genealogical Index* and its online cousin FamilySearch, which includes millions of names from both parish and nonconformist registers. The *IGI*, which is maintained by the Mormon LDS Church (see p. 21), covers only christenings and marriages, is by no means complete and contains many mistakes – but even so, it's a very useful tool and may well point you in the right direction. As well as being online (at www.familysearch. org), it is available on microfiche and CD-ROM.

The Federation of Family History Societies has recently published the first edition of the *National Burial Index*, which seeks to complement the *IGI* by indexing burial registers. Although coverage is patchy at present, it should increase greatly in future editions.

Nonconformists and Catholics

'George Whitfield preaching', by John Collet

During the 18th century more and more people were attracted by other faiths – especially Methodism, which seemed to be more vital than the Church of England and to answer doctrinal questions in a more contemporary way. In general nonconformists were tolerated, although only Anglicans could be officers in the armed forces or attend university. But the position was very different for Roman Catholics, who remained actively discriminated against until the end of the 18th century.

Many nonconformists continued to use parish churches for christenings, marriages and funerals in order to stay within the law. In addition, people sometimes changed from one denomination to another – for instance, a self-made businessman might start life as a Methodist but become a pillar of the Church of England once he had made his fortune.

Nonconformist records

On the setting up of the new central system of births, marriages and deaths in 1837, the government asked nonconformist churches to send in their registers, and most were happy to comply. These registers are now with the PRO, and copies can be seen at the Family Records Centre and in the Microfilm Reading Room at Kew. A central registry, at Dr Williams's Library in London, also kept details of vital events submitted by individuals and these records can now also be found on microfilm at the PRO and FRC.

Nonconformist registers for the period after 1837 have either been deposited with local record offices or retained by individual churches or chapels. Some transcripts have been made, and copies are often to be found at the Society of Genealogists.

Catholic records

Catholic churches were also asked to send in their registers but relatively few did so, and because of the illegality of Catholicism relatively few records survive. Most Catholic parish registers are still retained by the parish church. Details of fines and other penalties imposed upon Recusants (people who remained Catholics) are to be found at the PRO and in quarter sessions records at local record offices. The Society of Genealogists has transcripts of some parish records and other material about Catholics; and the Catholic Central Library has considerable resources, too.

Catholic births and baptisms register from Lawkland, Yorkshire, 1745–1840 (RG 4/2645)

Monumental inscriptions

Tombstones and the monuments inside churches can provide useful information about the deceased and their families. Fortunately you don't have to go to where your ancestors are buried to get this information, although such visits can be very moving. Most family history societies and a number of other organizations have visited local churches and graveyards and noted down details of inscriptions on tombstones and monuments. A national collection of these monumental inscriptions is held by the Society of Genealogists. Local studies libraries and archives should have copies for their areas.

Further reading

Michael Gandy, *Tracing Catholic Ancestors* (PRO, 2001)
Michael Gandy, *Tracing Nonconformist Ancestors* (PRO, 2001)
Jeremy Gibson, *Bishops' Transcripts and Marriage Licences, Bonds and Allegations* (FFHS, 2001)
Patrick Palgrave Moore, *Understanding the History and Records of Non-Conformity* (Elvery Dowers Publications, 1994)

Catholic Central Library

Lancing Street
London NW1 1ND
Tel: 020 7383 4333

You might also try

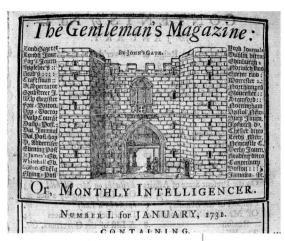

Gentleman's Magazine, 1731

The further back you go the more difficult it becomes to find the details you want, largely because there are far fewer documents, many of them having been lost over the centuries. If you can't find an ancestor in the parish registers or the various national indexes to them, you might try the following sources.

If your ancestor was poor:
• Parish Poor Law records (particularly church-wardens' accounts) itemize the payment of small sums or the provision of clothes and food to the elderly and the infirm and to the mothers of illegitimate children.

If your ancestor was well to do:
• Births, marriages and deaths often appeared in the *Gentleman's Magazine*, which was first published in 1732. There are indexes up to 1819. I have tracked down several of my ancestors in this way. Both the PRO Library and the SoG have sets of the magazine.
• Property deeds and related records often include copies of marriage settlements and other documents that provide clues about marriages. These records are normally at local record offices.
• The date a will was proved can give a rough idea when and perhaps where a person died. Also wills (see pp. 42–45) often mention members of the testator's family.

If you can't find the record of a marriage:

- Before 1754, to get around the need for banns and other regulations, many marriages were not performed in parish churches. The favourite place was the Fleet Prison, where by the 1740s half of London's marriages were being celebrated. It is thought that 230,000 marriages in total were celebrated in or about the prison. Legislation regarding marriages was tightened up by Hardwicke's Marriage Act of 1753, which stipulated that, except for Quakers and Jews, marriages had to take place in an Anglican church. Registers from the Fleet Prison and a few other centres can be consulted at the PRO and FRC.

- If the bride and groom did not live in the parish where they wanted to get married, or wanted to get married in a hurry, the parties could apply for a marriage licence from the bishop in the diocese where they lived. These licences are mostly to be found at local record offices. The SoG has indexes to licences issued by the Bishop of London and the Archbishop of Canterbury.

Fleet Prison, from 'London Life', c. 1807

FLEET PRISON

© Squash Bureau

THE CENSUS

Census records are some of the most important – and most interesting – records that you will use in researching your ancestors. These records offer a fascinating snapshot of your family and the way they lived on a specific night.

The first British census was held in 1801, and with the exception of 1941 there has been one every 10 years ever since. The first census legislation was passed by Parliament in November 1800 and the census was taken three months later – an incredibly short period of time. Local officials found that 9 million people lived in England and Wales, but we do not who they were as few names or other individual details were collected. This was the pattern of the census until 1841.

By the late 1830s the Royal Statistical Society and others were pressing for more detailed questions, but there was considerable opposition from people who feared infringement of their civil liberties. The first census to contain details of every individual in Great Britain was taken in 1841. Because of these initial fears, it is less informative than later ones. More detailed questions were included in 1851 and in subsequent censuses.

A few days before census night officials known as enumerators distributed questionnaires to heads of household (normally the senior male), who was expected to complete them. They returned a few days later to collect the completed forms and help those who were illiterate to fill them in. Once all the questionnaires had been collected, the information was entered into books and the books were sent to Whitehall for processing. It is these census enumerators' books that survive. With just a few exceptions, the original forms have been destroyed.

The census provides information about family servants as well as direct ancestors (COPY 1/443)

Where to go and what to do

Census returns are closed to public access for 100 years to protect confidentiality – so census records for 1841 to 1891 are currently available and the records for 1901 are released in January 2002. The censuses from before 1841 have been destroyed.

The Family Records Centre has a set of census records from 1841 to 1891 for England, Wales, the Channel Islands and the Isle of Man; and most local archives and libraries have copies of the census for their area.

The 1901 census will be available from January 2002 in two ways:

- There will be access to the 1901 census on the internet, at www.census.pro.gov.uk. The website will offer digitized images of the census itself (for a fee) and will include a free index.

- Sets of microfiche will be viewable at the Public Record Office in Kew (but not at the FRC) and at local libraries and archives.

If you are not sure where to begin your search, start with the 1881 census – for which a full surname index exists both on CD-ROM (as a fully searchable database) and on microfiche. It gives you almost all the information you would find on the original documents, together with the PRO reference to enable you to look at the film at the Family Records Centre. Errors, however, do occur. The German radical Karl Marx, for example, is indexed as Karl Wass!

Census records are arranged by the enumerators' districts. This can make finding an individual family difficult. But if you know where they lived on census night, there are street indexes at the Family Records Centre for London and many of the larger towns.

Family completing the census, from George Sims' *Living London,* **1901**

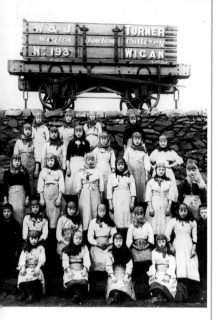

The census gives valuable information on occupations. Pit girls, 1893 (COPY 1/412)

Many family history societies have prepared surname indexes for their areas, particularly for the 1851 census, and the FRC has a large collection of these booklets.

Each CEB (census enumerator's book) is arranged in the same way. At the front is a description of the area covered, followed by a printed example (beware, many people assume that this is part of the actual returns). The entries are arranged according to the way the enumerator issued and collected the questionnaires. Consequently a long street may appear several times in a book, and perhaps be covered by three or four books.

Entries may look as if they have been scored out (this was done in London by the clerks who were analysing the returns), which can make them difficult to read. If you have problems, ask the staff for help: they normally have a great deal of experience of deciphering handwriting.

There are various other problems with the census:

- Between 5 and 10 per cent of the 1861 census is missing, as is a small part of 1851.
- For one reason or another, about 5 per cent of the population do not appear in the census – perhaps because they were not at home or the enumerator forgot to include them, or because they were sleeping rough.
- There are errors in individual entries. The age is often a year or two out, either because people did not know their correct age or did not want it to be known. The occupation given can be misleading, and it can be difficult to work out where people were born (either the details are incomplete or the

parish given does not exist – often because the enumerator misheard what he was being told).

- In Victorian times, people moved home far more frequently than one might suppose. However, the chances are that they remained in the same neighbourhood – so if there is no trace of them at the expected address on census night, it may be worth checking to see if they were elsewhere in the area.

Other sources

Much of the information contained in the census returns is unique and cannot be found elsewhere. The nearest equivalent is the published street directories (see p. 60) – which list all but the poorest householders year by year, together with their trade or occupation, although only the (normally male) head of the household figures in these directories. They can also be useful in tracking down people who have moved, and so do not appear at the expected address in the census.

Further reading

David Annal, *Using Census Records* (PRO, revised edition 2001)

Jeremy Gibson and Elizabeth Hampson, *Census Returns, 1841–1891, in Microform: a Directory to Local Holdings in Great Britain* (FFHS, 3rd edition 1997)

Jeremy Gibson, *Local Census Listings, 1522–1930* (FFHS, 3rd edition 1997)

Edward Higgs, *Making Sense of the Census* (HMSO, 1989)

Susan Lumas, *An Introduction to Census Records* (FFHS, 1992)

Public Record Office, *FRC Introduction to Family History* (PRO, 1999)

About 5 per cent of the population – including those who were sleeping rough – do not appear in the census (COPY 1/460)

What the census can reveal

As well as telling you about your direct ancestors, census records can provide other information, such as:

- Details about relatives, lodgers and servants resident in the household or staying there on census night.
- If relatives of the wife were at the house on census night (and this is normally clear from the column giving relationship to the householder), you may discover the wife's maiden name and perhaps some details about her relatives as well.
- The birthplaces given for the children sometimes enable you to track the movement of a family around the country.
- Using the information in the birthplace column for the adults, you can go to the relevant parish registers to track down information about their christenings (see pp. 30–31).

How the records relate to your ancestors

The answers people provided to the questions give valuable information about themselves and other members of their family. In addition, they may lead you to other records – either to find out more about the people in the census or to take your search further back in time.

You can discover the following:

Edward VII and family (COPY 1/183)

Their full name

Their sex

Their marital state

Their age

(In the 1841 census, for adults over 15 years old this was rounded down to the nearest five years. If you were aged 47 on census night, you would therefore be entered as being 45.)

Their relationship to the head of the household

(Normally deemed to be the oldest man.)

1891 census return for the parish of Sandringham, Norfolk (RG 12/1564)

Administrative County of *Norfolk*						The undermention
Civil Parish		Municipal Borough		Municipal Ward		Urban S-
of *Sandringham*						

Cols. 1	2	3	4	5	6	7	CO.
No. of Schedule	ROAD, STREET, &c., and No. or NAME of HOUSE	HOUSES In-habit-ed	Unin-habited (U.), or Building (B.)	Number of rooms occupied if less than five	NAME and Surname of each Person	RELATION to Head of Family	DIT- as Mar-
9	*Park House Cott.*	1			*Charlotte Sophie Noedel*	*Head*	*S*
	Technical School						
					Emma Jane Sayer	*Serv*	*S*
10	*Rectory Cottage*	1		4	*John Steel*	*Head*	*M*
					Elizabeth Do	*Wife*	*M*
					Ellen L. Do	*Daur*	
					Francis L. Do	*Son*	
					Horace I. T. Do	*Do*	
11	*The Rectory*	1			*Frederick A. J. Hervey*	*Head*	*M*
					Mabel E. Do	*Wife*	*M*
					Alexandra L. Do	*Daur*	
					Emma Spratt	*Serv*	*S*
					Ruth Smith	*Do*	*S*
					Emily R. Cock	*Do*	*W*
12	*Sandringham House*	1			*Albert Edward The Prince of Wales*	*Head*	*M*
					Alexandra the Princess of Wales	*Wife*	*M*
					Princess Victoria of Wales	*Daur*	*S*
					Princess Maud of Do	*Do*	*S*
					Do Margaret of Prussia	*Niece*	*S*
					The Duke of Cambridge	*Cousin*	*S*
					The Lady Suffield		*M*
					The Honble Lady Knollys	*Visitor*	*M*
					Sir Francis Knollys		*M*
4	Total of Houses and of Tenements with less than Five Rooms	4	1		Total of Males and Females		

NOTE.—Draw the pen through such of the words of the headings as are inappropriate.

Their occupation
(Which can be misleading. Very few prostitutes are included, although there were tens of thousands of women engaged in 'the oldest trade'; and children were commonly entered as 'scholars' even though they may not have been at school.)

Their birthplace
(In the 1841 census this was noted simply as being within the county or outside it. From 1851 the parish and county of birth had to be given. For people born in Scotland or Ireland or abroad, it was sufficient to put the country of birth.)

within the Boundaries of the		Page 2		
Town or Village or Hamlet	Rural Sanitary District	Parliamentary Borough or Division	Ecclesiastical Parish or District	
Sandringham	of Freebridge Lynn	of North West Norfolk	of Sandringham	

11	12	13	14	15	16
PROFESSION or OCCUPATION	Employer	Employed	Neither Employer nor Employed	WHERE BORN	If (1) Deaf-and-Dumb (2) Blind (3) Lunatic, Imbecile or Idiot
Lady Superintend.t of Her R. & The Princess of Wales' Technical School	X			Germany	
General Servant Dom				Norfolk. Sandringham	
Groom & Gardener				Do. Burn Farm	
				Do. Babingley	
Scholar				Do. West Newton	
				Do. Babingley	
				Do. Sandringham	
Rector & Domestic Chaplain to H.R.H. Prince of Wales	X			London. St James' Sq.	
				Malta (British subject)	
				London. 12 Lowndes St	
Lady's maid				Norfolk. Wiggenhall St M	
Cook Dom				" West Newton	
Parlour Maid				" Norwich	
do in.	X			London. Buckingham palace	✓
				Denmark (British Subject) nat	
				London. Marlbro Ho.	
				Do. Do.	
				Germany.	
Army				Do. (British Subject)	✓
Lady in Waiting to the Princess of Wales				Madeira. (Do.) Port	✓
				Norfolk. Ashwell Thorp	
Private Secy to H.R.H. The Prince of Wales	X			London. N K	✓

Eng.—Sheet B.

Who was living at the house on census night
(Even if they did not normally live there. For people at sea or travelling overnight by train, they will either be enumerated at the address they arrived at next morning or, in 1871, on board ship)

Whether they were blind, deaf, dumb or insane
In addition, in 1891 and 1901 people had to indicate:

Whether they were employed, self-employed or unemployed.
(This question was often misunderstood, so the answers are unreliable.)

In Wales, whether they spoke Welsh, Welsh and English, or just English.

WHERE THERE'S A WILL THERE'S A WAY

Will of David Garrick (PROB 1/16)

Wills can provide a useful source for family history – describing the property and possessions held by the maker of the will, listing members of the family, friends and, on occasion, servants, and sometimes indicating what he or she thought of them. Shakespeare, for example, left his second best bed to his wife, although this wasn't meant to be an insult – it apparently was quite a common thing to do at the time. Wills are, of course, important legal documents and may be consulted generations after the death of the will maker in order to discern their instructions about the establishment or purpose of a trust or charity. Which is why so many survive.

Until fairly recently, however, wills were made by a relatively small proportion of the population (a survey suggested that in 1900 only about one in ten people made a will). Most individuals had so little to leave that their possessions were divided up among their family without the involvement of the law; and wills were generally made when the individual – in legal terminology, the testator (male) or testatrix (female) – was either very old or seriously ill.

The earliest wills date from the 14th century. The basic form has changed little since then, although modern wills are unlikely to include instructions for masses to be said in the testator's name or commend the individual's soul to God's mercy. Before 1733 they were usually in Latin (as were most legal documents), but with a little practice it is fairly easy to pick out the key points.

Until 1884, all the property belonging to a woman passed to her husband when she married – so before then there are wills for spinsters and widows, but not for married women.

Wills from 1858 onwards

In January 1858 a system similar to the registration of births, marriages and deaths was introduced, with a network of district probate registries channelling wills to the Principal Probate Registry in London. Once a will has been 'proved', it becomes a public record and can be consulted by anyone.

In 1998, the Principal Probate Registry moved from Somerset House to the address shown opposite. The Probate Searchroom there is open to the public from 10 a.m to 4.30 p.m., Monday to Friday. No appointment is necessary, but a fee, currently £5, is charged for each will produced. You can order copies of wills while you are at the registry. Information about the system and the fees payable can be found at www.courtservice.gov.uk/fandl/prob_guidance.htm or in leaflets obtainable from the principal and district probate registries.

Calendars (registers) are provided for each year. They list all wills proved and give a reference number which you quote if you decide to order a will. The calendars state the value of the estate and who the executors (normally members of the family) were. Otherwise, they include much the same information as a death certificate does. And it's free! Copies of the calendars on microfiche, between 1858 and 1943, are available in the Microfilm Reading Room at the PRO, Kew and at the FRC.

There are also thirteen district probate registries, which have calendars going back 50 years as well as copies of wills proved locally.

You can order copies of wills by post from the York Probate Sub-Registry. For a postal search, the fee is £5 per three-year period, plus the charge for a copy of the will itself.

The PRO is undertaking a project to make scanned images of many PCC wills available online for a fee. Initially this will be for wills proved between 1850 and 1858. For further details visit www.pro.gov.uk/online/pro-online.htm.

David Garrick as Richard III, by William Hogarth, 1745

Principal Probate Registry

First Avenue House
42–9 High Holborn
London WC1V 6NP
Tel: 020 7947 6000

Postal Searches and Copies Department

York Probate Sub-Registry

Duncombe Place
York YO1 7EA

Wills before 1858

Death of Little Nell, from Dickens' *The Old Curiosity Shop*

Finding wills before 1858 is, frankly, a minefield. It may be the most complicated research you undertake, but the results can be very rewarding. There are at least four places where you might find a will, largely because probate was administered by a complex network of ecclesiastical courts (since a will was regarded as a contract between the testator and God). Where a will was proved depended basically on how rich the deceased was. Surviving records are at a number of county record offices as well as at the FRC and the PRO.

The PRO has the records of the Prerogative Court of Canterbury (PCC) – the supreme ecclesiastical court, which covered the whole of England and Wales. If property was held both north and south of the River Trent or in two or more dioceses south of the river, then the PCC was the court where the will had to be proved. It also exercised jurisdiction over the estates of those who died abroad.

Executors often had wills proved in courts higher than necessary. During the first half of the 19th century there was a growing tendency to use the PCC for even relatively small wills, including those made by soldiers and sailors. The records themselves are available on microfilm at both the PRO and the FRC. There are a number of indexes of varying usefulness to PCC wills, including several detailed series for the 18th century compiled by the Friends of the PRO. Copies of these indexes can also be found at the Society of Genealogists.

The other archbishop's court was the Prerogative Court of York (PCY), which covered England north of the River Trent. Its records are at The Borthwick Institute of Historical Research.

Again, there are indexes that can help you track down your ancestors. There was also a network of diocesan and archdeaconry courts, which mostly proved wills of lesser amount. Their records are usually held by county record offices.

For about a century after 1670 the convention was for the will to be accompanied by an inventory listing all the items belonging to the deceased room by room, including the contents of outhouses and farm buildings etc. From these inventories you can get a very good idea of how a house was furnished and the resources the individual had to make his way in the world.

Grants of admission

An administration is a legal arrangement which enables the estate of someone who died intestate (that is without making a will) to be wound up. Under such circumstances, it is usual for an adult next of kin – frequently the spouse – to apply to the probate court for letters of administration (often abbreviated to 'admons'). Before 1815 grants were normally only applied for if large sums of money were involved and the family could not come to an amicable private arrangement. These records tend to be disappointing, as they often give only the name and address of the deceased and of the person to whom the admon was granted.

Further reading

Audrey Collins, *Using Wills after 1858 and First Avenue House* (FFHS, 1998)

Jane Cox, *Wills, Probate and Death Duties* (FFHS, 1993)

Jeremy Gibson, *Probate Jurisdictions: Where to look for wills* (FFHS, 1994)

Karen Grannum, *Using Wills* (PRO, revised edition 2001)

Miriam Scott, *Prerogative Court of Canterbury: Wills and Other Probate Records* (PRO, 1997)

The Borthwick Institute of Historical Research
Peaseholme Green
York YO1 2PW
Internet: www.york.ac.uk/inst/bihr/

DIVORCE RECORDS

One in three marriages now end in divorce. This statistic would have shocked our ancestors, for whom divorce was both rare and expensive.

A trial in the divorce courts, from George Sims' *Living London*, 1901

Principal Registry of the Family Division

First Avenue House
42–9 High Holborn
London WC1V 6NP

Until after the Second World War, if you had irreconcilable differences with your partner you generally either endured a joyless marriage or deserted your family to 'live in sin' with another person. In fact, cohabitation seems to have been far more common than is supposed, although it was usually kept a close secret for fear of what the neighbours would think. In extreme cases, it was not unknown for men to offer their wives for sale in markets.

Until 1858 the only way to obtain a formal divorce was by an act of Parliament. However, ways emerged to get round this. The most common resort was for the man to desert his family. As this was a private matter, there are rarely any formal records, except for the occasional petition (among the quarter sessions records) for maintenance from the deserted wife. If the couple were well-to-do, there might be a private deed of separation between the husband and the trustee of the wife, the latter having no legal existence in common law. These deeds can be found in the close rolls and other Chancery Court records. An alternative was to seek judicial separation from an ecclesiastical court; and there are various series of records at the PRO which contain such material.

The Matrimonial Causes Act 1857 established the first divorce courts, although the grounds for divorce were not made much easier, particularly for women. Divorce court files from 1858 to 1943 are at the PRO (although from 1938 to 1943 only samples from the files have survived). Because so few divorces took place, the proceedings are also often covered, in detail, in the newspapers.

Divorce was liberalized in several stages after the Second World War. Copies of decrees nisi and absolute can be obtained from the Principal Registry of the Family Division. The PRO has a small sample of these records.

MILITARY RECORDS BEFORE 1914

Some of the most popular records at the PRO relate to the Army and the Navy. During the 18th and 19th centuries tens of thousands of men served in the armed forces, and the records they left behind offer a great deal of valuable information, particularly about those who served in the Army.

Britain's armed services have always been small. In 1899, at the height of British imperial power, there were just 180,000 officers and other ranks in the Army and 93,000 officers and ratings in the Navy. Army personnel tended to alternate between service in the British Isles and tours of duty in the Empire, particularly India. In addition, there was a separate Indian Army. But the real defensive force was the Royal Navy – as the original Articles of War put it, 'It is upon the Navy that under the good providence of God the wealth, prosperity and peace of these Islands and of the Empire do mainly depend.'

Conditions could be harsh. In the Army barracks were overcrowded and squalid, and the diet meagre. During the 1850s, for example, the standard diet consisted of a daily ration of a pound of bread, eaten at breakfast with coffee, and three quarters of a pound of meat boiled for midday dinner in large coppers in cookhouses. Life was made bearable by companionship and drink, and few soldiers managed to remain undisciplined for drunkenness during their service. From the 1860s, however, due to pressure from civilian groups and the difficulties of recruiting sufficient men, conditions began to improve.

The more information you have before you start,

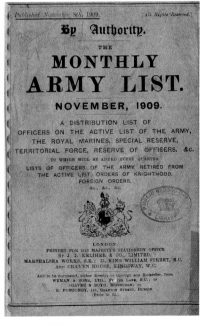

Published November 8th, 1909. *[All Rights Reserved.]*

By Authority.

THE

MONTHLY ARMY LIST.

NOVEMBER, 1909.

A DISTRIBUTION LIST OF
OFFICERS ON THE ACTIVE LIST OF THE ARMY,
THE ROYAL MARINES, SPECIAL RESERVE,
TERRITORIAL FORCE, RESERVE OF OFFICERS, &c.
TO WHICH WILL BE ADDED EVERY QUARTER
LISTS OF OFFICERS OF THE ARMY RETIRED FROM
THE ACTIVE LIST, ORDERS OF KNIGHTHOOD,
FOREIGN ORDERS,
&c., &c., &c.

LONDON:
PRINTED FOR HIS MAJESTY'S STATIONERY OFFICE
By J. J. KELIHER & CO., LIMITED,
MARSHALSEA WORKS, S.E. ; 33, KING WILLIAM STREET, E.C.
AND CRAVEN HOUSE, KINGSWAY, W.C.

And to be purchased, either directly or through any Bookseller, from
WYMAN & SONS, LTD., FETTER LANE, E.C. ; or
OLIVER & BOYD, EDINBURGH; or
E. PONSONBY, 116, GRAFTON STREET, DUBLIN.
[Price 1s. 6d.]

The *Army List* includes the names of all officers

Officers' records at the PRO

Published lists All officers are included in the *Army List* – where you should be able to find details of promotions and the unit or units your ancestor served with, and sometimes brief details of the campaigns in which he served. *Hart's Army List*, a rival publication which first appeared in 1839, also contains biographical information. Both can be found in the Microfilm Reading Room at the PRO.

Service records There are five series containing officers' records. To find out which records are in which series, consult the comprehensive card index in the PRO's Research Enquiries Room.

Commissions The correspondence about the purchase and sale of commissions between 1793 and 1871 contains plenty of valuable genealogical material.

Pensions There are registers and correspondence about the payment of pensions up to 1921, including some records for pensions paid to widows and children.

the easier your search will be. In particular you need to have an idea of which unit a man served with – that is with which regiment or corps in the Army, or ship in the Navy. This is very important if you are trying to trace men who left the forces before the middle of the 19th century, as the service records are largely organized by unit.

It is also important to know whether they were officers or ordinary soldiers or sailors, for the records of officers and other ranks are very different. If you are not sure, check in the *Army List* or *Navy List*, which include all officers. There are copies in the Microfilm Reading Room at the PRO; and some libraries have copies, too.

Army

To appreciate how your soldier ancestor fitted into the scheme of things, you need to have a grasp of the organization of the Army. Traditionally the most important unit has been the regiment for the infantry, guards and cavalry; and the corps for the artillery and engineers. The peacetime regiment normally consisted of two or more battalions, each comprising perhaps 1,000 men. Often one battalion was stationed abroad, while the rest of the regiment remained in Britain, recruiting and training troops.

Officers largely came from the landed classes, who had the private income to pay for entertaining and the uniforms. Before the First World War perhaps four or five officers each year were promoted from the ranks, the most famous being William Robertson who joined the Lincolnshire Regiment as a private in the 1870s and rose to the rank of Field Marshal. Officers were generally poorly trained and learnt their military skills during colonial campaigns, but by the end of the 19th century the Army Staff College was beginning to turn out more professional officers.

Enlistment for the other ranks was traditionally for a period of 21 years. In an attempt to make the Army more attractive to potential recruits, enlistment was cut to six years in the 1870s. Before that time desertion was common, as many men found they could not endure the harsh conditions and lengthy period of service.

Ordinary soldiers tended to come from the poorest strata of society. During the Napoleonic Wars, the Duke of Wellington famously described his troops as being the 'scum of the earth'. He then went on: 'People talk of their enlisting from fine military feeling – all stuff – no such thing. Some of the men enlist from having got bastard children – some for minor offences – many more for drink; it is really a wonder that we should make them the fine fellows they are.'

Further reading

Simon Fowler and William Spencer, *Army Service Records for Family Historians* (PRO, 1998)

William Spencer, *Using Army Records* (PRO, new edition 2001)

Records for other ranks at the PRO

Service records There are two series of records for men who survived to receive a pension. Before 1883 these records are arranged by regiment, although a name index to records before 1854 is in the PRO's Microfilm Reading Room. The documents indicate when and where a man served, place and age on enlistment, disciplinary offences, promotions, and reason for discharge. They sometimes list wives and children.

Muster rolls These list every man in a regiment, including officers, and were compiled monthly. They indicate a man's pay, any offences committed during the previous month, and the location of the regiment. They begin in 1732 and end in 1898.

Pensions Men who left the Army after serving their time or as the result of wounds were entitled to a pension from the Royal Hospital, Chelsea. Most of these were 'out-pensioners', meaning that they received their pension at home. There are a variety of records listing pensions paid.

Medals The PRO has medal rolls for campaigns from the Battle of Waterloo onwards, listing both officers and other ranks entitled to medals.

Army barracks during the Boer War, March 1900 (COPY 1/445)

Officers' records at the PRO

Published lists **All naval officers are included in the** *Navy List*, **and it is possible to trace promotions and ships served on from these lists.**

Service records **These exist for officers after 1840, although there are some retrospective entries back to 1756. These records will give you the ships served on, promotions, some personal details and those of any spouse.**

Passing certificates **One interesting source is the passing certificates that were issued to prove qualifications of officers. These include details of service and some personal information.**

Royal Navy

Conditions were no better in the Royal Navy than in the Army. Until the 1850s, when a permanent career structure was introduced, men signed on for specific voyages – so might well serve on both Royal Navy and merchant ships – and officers might spend much of their time ashore on half pay, waiting for postings.

It's fair to say that the methods employed by the Navy during the Napoleonic wars had evolved so little over the previous two centuries that a sailor who fought against the Spanish Armada in 1588 would have noticed little difference at the Battle of Trafalgar. But this would soon change. During the 19th century the Navy's equipment and tactics were revolutionized: steam replaced wind power, the screw propeller supplanted the sail, bigger and better guns were introduced, and wireless telegraphy transformed how ships communicated.

Conditions for ratings also improved. Under Nelson, standard rations were based on hard ship's biscuits and salted beef and pork, all of which could be years old, while breakfast consisted of a mixture of oatmeal and molasses known as 'burgoo'. Fresh vegetables and fruit were provided, to stave off scurvy, but could be hard to come by on long missions in foreign waters. By the First World War conditions had improved considerably, and the larger ships might even have their own bakeries.

Until the 1850s, a sailor's period of service might last between five and seven years. There was little chance of promotion; in particular, for an ordinary sailor to be commissioned as an officer was a very rare occurrence. The gulf between officers and men was

HMS *Victory* and HMS *Majestic*, 1899 (COPY 1/150)

every bit as great as in the Army. Again, this was largely the result of the different social backgrounds – the aristocracy and middle classes providing the officers, and the working class the ratings.

Further reading

Bruno Pappalardo, *Using Naval Records* (PRO, revised edition 2001)

N.A.M. Rodger, *Naval Records for Family Historians* (PRO, 1998)

You might also try

By far the largest proportion of personnel records relating to the services are with the PRO. The National Army Museum and regimental museums may on occasion be able to provide information regarding soldiers (particularly officers). Similarly, the National Maritime Museum and the Royal Naval Museum may be of help for naval officers and ratings. Addresses for these museums are given on p. 79.

The Society of Genealogists' library (see p. 79) has a fair collection of printed material, including medal rolls, casualty lists and biographies for both services.

The annual *Family and Local History Handbook* (see p. 80) contains addresses for many regimental museums.

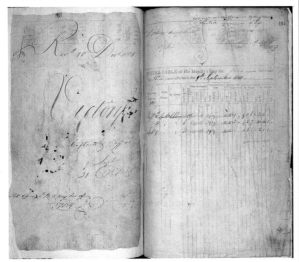

Muster book of HMS *Victory*, 1805 (ADM 36/15900)

Records for ratings at the PRO

Before 1853 There were no service records for ratings until 1853. Men were discharged at the end of each voyage, so there was no continuity of service. There are, however, three places to look:

- For men who retired with a pension between 1802 and 1894, there are their certificates of service, which list the ships served on and dates of service.
- Ships' muster and pay books will tell you when a sailor enlisted and his age and place of birth.
- Ships' logbooks can be of help on occasion and of course provide information about the voyages themselves.

Service records In 1853 a new series of continuous service engagement books was introduced for ratings, and this formed the basis of service records until 1923. After 1894, however, you will have to know which branch of the Navy, such as engineers or armament, your ancestor served with. These records normally include dates of entry and discharge, ships served on, promotions, any disciplinary offences and some personal details.

Medal rolls These rolls include awards for gallantry and campaign medals, both for officers and ratings.

MILITARY RECORDS FROM 1914 ONWARDS

If any of your relatives were in the services during either of the two world wars or other of the conflicts of the 20th century, you should be able to find out about them at the Public Record Office.

The Commonwealth War Graves Commission

If you are trying to trace members of your family who lost their lives during the two world wars, the Commonwealth War Graves Commission can help you. Their database will tell you where a person is buried, and provide information such as his or her unit, regimental number and date of death. The database is available online at www.cwgc.org.uk. You can also write to them at

Commonwealth War Graves Commission

2 Marlow Road
Maidenhead SL6 7DX
Tel: 01628 34221

Service records for men who were in the forces up to the end of 1920 are now very largely available and provide a fascinating and at times moving insight into the lives of the soldiers, sailors and airmen who served in these wars. Although service records have not yet been released for the Second World War, you can use unit records to find out what your relatives did.

Before you start your research, you to need to know:

- Whether your ancestor was an officer, non-commissioned officer (corporal or sergeant) or other rank (rating in the Royal Navy). All commissioned officers (lieutenants, captains and the like) are listed in the *Army*, *Navy* and *Air Force Lists*, which can be consulted in the Microfilm Reading Room at the PRO. Large libraries may also have sets. So if you are not sure, it is easy to check.
- The name of the unit your ancestor served with – usually the battalion in the Army, ship in the Royal Navy, or squadron in the RAF. You can manage without this information in initial searches among the records of the First World War (although it can be extremely useful), but for the Second World War it is essential.

Further reading

William Spencer, *Army Service Records of the First World War* (PRO, 3rd edition 2001)

William Spencer, *Air Force Records for Family Historians* (PRO, 2000)

Readers may also wish to consult an article by Stephen Smith describing the main sources for the Navy during the First World War, in *Family History Monthly*, August 2001.

First World War

Army

In the war cemetery at St Symphorien, near Mons in Belgium, can be seen the graves of the first and last British soldiers killed during the First World War. Private J. Parr of the Middlesex Regiment and Private G.E. Ellison of the 5th Royal Irish Lancers are buried almost opposite each other. For many this coincidence symbolizes the waste and sacrifice of the Great War – especially since the first and last skirmishes involving British forces also took place locally, no great distance from one another.

During the First World War, 6,000,000 men and a few women served in the armed services; 5,250,000 (just under half of whom were volunteers) served in the Army; 450,000 were in the Royal Navy; and 300,000 in the Royal Air Force. Of this number, 723,000 lost their lives and another 1,663,000 were wounded. When you consider that nearly one in seven of the British population saw military service, it is little wonder that the relevant service records have, since their release a few years ago, become among the most frequently used material at the PRO.

The story these records tell is very different to the popular image of the war. Although conditions in the front line were grim, most infantrymen and artillerymen saw front-line action for only relatively short periods, with long spells of training and rest. Indeed many of the men serving in support units may never have seen a shot fired in anger.

Graves of Private J. Parr and Private G.E. Ellison

For family historians, there are three main sources for the First World War:

Service records Some 60 per cent of the service records of men who served between 1914 and the end of 1920 were destroyed by fire in 1940. The surviving records may give place and date of enlistment, medical information, disciplinary offences and other details, but what is in each document varies greatly. Because of their great fragility, this material is available on microfilm only. About 85 per cent of the service records for officers survive – but unfortunately they are not as informative as the records for the other ranks, as they are largely concerned with pensions claims.

Medal record cards If you can't find a service record or are not sure of the unit a person served with, the microfilmed medal record cards are a particularly useful source. Men who served overseas were awarded at least two campaign medals. Their award was recorded on these cards, which will tell you the regiment(s) a man served with, the medals he was entitled to, and roughly where he served.

War diaries These are a record of activities and occurrences day by day of units that saw service overseas. Descriptions are usually quite brief and, particularly if written in the heat of battle, may be scrawled in pencil. Officers are often referred to by name, but it is rare for individual soldiers to be mentioned. Nevertheless, they provide a first-hand account of the daily life of the unit.

The record sources are as follows:

Service records There are separate series for officers and ratings. For each man, they give date of birth, ship or shore establishment, and a concise account of service, including successive appointments. In the officers' records, there are some interesting confidential reports on individuals. This series also includes records for Royal Marines officers, while records of ordinary marines can be found elsewhere.

Log books These normally record only navigational and meteorological information, so for the most part won't tell you very much about an individual's life on board ship. However, captains also submitted detailed reports about any actions they had been involved in.

Medal rolls There are medal rolls for both officers and men.

Royal Navy

At the outbreak of war, the Royal Navy was the most powerful in the world. However, apart from the inconclusive Battle of Jutland in 1916, it rarely saw direct action against the enemy. By 1917 most of its efforts were directed to protecting convoys of ships bringing vital supplies to Britain across the Atlantic. Some 50,000 naval ratings and their officers also served in Royal Naval Divisions on the Western Front – where they maintained distinct naval discipline, and the officers retained their beards much to the annoyance of their clean-shaven Army colleagues.

Navy Recruitment
Poster, 1917
(ADM 1/8331)

Royal Air Force

The Royal Air Force was formed on 1 April 1918, out of the Royal Flying Corps (RFC) and Royal Naval Air Service (RNAS). At the outbreak of the war, flying was still very much in its infancy; by the Armistice it had become an important part of the war machine. The public lapped up stories of chivalrous and heroic air aces, in stark contrast to the stalemate on the Western Front. However, the aviators' effectiveness was compromised by rivalry and duplication of effort between the RFC and RNAS. The RAF successfully merged all these air activities together under one command.

Service records For men who served only in the RFC and RNAS, see Army and Navy records respectively. RAF officers' records contain details of units served with, promotions, next of kin, and often caustic comments from superior officers on flying abilities. These records are available on microfilm, although alternate pages have been filmed upside down. You need a good sense of navigation to use them successfully! Similar, but correctly filmed, records exist for other ranks.

Operation record books These record daily activities, including flights undertaken. Their survival is a bit patchy, and what they contain varies considerably from squadron to squadron.

Medal cards and rolls RFC and RAF officers and men are listed in the medal records cards, while details of RNAS campaign medals can be found in the Navy medal rolls.

Correspondence There is a series of correspondence, which is an intriguing hotchpotch of material. In it you may find such things as lists of personal possessions for airmen who had been shot down, and notes dropped by German pilots about British aviators whose machines had crashed on enemy soil and who had been taken prisoner.

**W.P. Mansbridge,
Royal Flying Corps
(RAIL 253/516)**

Operations Record Book,
440 Squadron, RCAF (AIR 27/1880)

Service records

Operational records relating to the Second World War are now available at the PRO. What has yet to be released are the service records – they are closed for 75 years. The Ministry of Defence will, however, release some details to former servicemen and next of kin, for which a fee is charged (currently £25). If you wish to have a search conducted, contact one of the following addresses for details:

Army

Ministry of Defence
CS(R)2B
Bourne Ave
Hayes
UB3 1RF

Royal Navy

Ministry of Defence
CS(R)2B
Bourne Ave
Hayes
UB3 1RF

RAF

Ministry of Defence
P MAN 2b(1),
RAF PMC HQ PTC,
RAF Innsworth,
Gloucester
GL3 1EZ

Second World War

In contrast to the First World War, which had been largely a static affair fought out in the trenches of France and Flanders, the Second World War was extraordinarily mobile, from the Blitzkrieg of May 1940 to the crossing of the Rhine nearly five years later. It was also a war of new technologies, such as radar, the jet engine and ultimately, of course, the atomic bomb. The British Army was a much smaller body than it had been a generation previously. For the first time, many more soldiers were involved in supporting the infantry than saw action themselves – what Churchill called the 'fluff and flummery behind the fighting troops'. The RAF came into its own, firstly during the Battle of Britain and then during the strategic bombing offensive over Germany. Its clean-shaven young pilots again became heroes in popular mythology. The Navy too did sterling if less romantic work, escorting convoys across the Atlantic and the Mediterranean and supporting the great landings in Normandy and Sicily.

Medals

Gallantry awards (the Victoria Cross and Military Medal etc.) are listed in the *London Gazette*, and indexes to them can be found in the PRO's Microfilm Reading Room. There are several series of records for each of the services. No campaign medal records from the Second World War have as yet been transferred to the PRO.

Roll of Honour

A list of men and women who died during the war is to be found in the PRO series WO 304. It is also available on CD-ROM in the PRO Library and in other libraries.

Further reading

There is no book on the Second World War written solely with family historians in mind, but there are relevant sections in:

Simon Fowler and William Spencer, *Army Records for Family Historians* (PRO, 1998)

Imperial War Museum, *Tracing your Family History: Army* (IWM, 2000)

Imperial War Museum, *Tracing your Family History: Royal Navy* (IWM, 2000)

Simon Fowler et al, *RAF Records in the PRO* (PRO, 1994)

Imperial War Museum, *Tracing your Family History: Royal Air Force* (IWM, 2000)

William Spencer, *Air Force Records for Family Historians* (PRO, 2000)

Second World War illustration of flying boat over merchant ship convoy (INF 3/1522)

Airman, 277 Squadron, RAF (AIR 27/1491)

Operational records

Army The main sources are the war diaries, which tend to be more informative and easier to use than their First World War equivalents. Genealogists may find the appendices useful, as they often include the orders that regulated day-to-day life in the unit and may note the arrival and departure of personnel at all ranks. The diaries are in various series arranged by theatre of operations.

Navy Log books normally merely record navigational and weather details. A more useful source are the reports submitted by captains to the Admiralty about operations, including reports from individual convoys.

Royal Air Force Operation record books (ORBs) are among my favourite records. They can offer a real insight into life in the RAF – from the price of prostitutes in France in 1939 to the appalling losses suffered by bomber squadrons. ORBs contain a monthly summary of notable events, plus a record of every flight made by the squadron and details of the aircraft and crews.

PRINTED SOURCES

This section deals with what historians call secondary or printed sources – that is material of which there is more than one copy, such as books, newspapers and directories.

Browne's General Law List 1799; *Richmond District Directory* 1901; *Kelly's Directory of Andover* 1956

You might think your ancestors were not at all special and so unlikely to appear in print – but you could be surprised. And if you find old documents difficult to decipher, it will no doubt be a relief to turn to printed sources.

Ever since newspapers were first published they've included stories about individuals, not just the famous and infamous but ordinary people too. Directories listing people by occupation or where they lived can be a useful way of checking or confirming information about an ancestor. Maps are an often ignored source, but can indicate where forebears lived or how much land they owned and perhaps describe the house they lived in.

Newspapers

You never know what you're going to find in old newspapers – which makes them both a joy and a curse to use. It is all too easy to be sidetracked by odd news stories, or advertisements for patent medicines. Indeed the biggest problem is the vast amount of information you may have to sift through before you find the item you're looking for.

The first newspapers were published in the mid 17th century. However, although they carried lots of stories about unusual phenomena, their news content was often culled from other sources. The newspaper as we know it today is really a product of the 19th century. The telegraph meant that news stories could be up-to-date. Better printing presses meant more and cheaper newspapers. By 1900 the first 'picture newspapers' – including the *Daily Mail* and *Daily Mirror* – were published, with a mass audience in mind. The mid 19th century saw the rise of the 'local rag', and most towns soon had two or three rival papers.

The Public Record Office has very few newspapers, although a set of *The Times* on microfilm can be found in the Microfilm Reading Room. Most local studies libraries will have newspapers for their area, usually on microfilm.

Very few newspapers have been indexed, so it is important that you have a rough idea when the event you are looking for occurred. The major exception is *The Times*, for which there is a widely available index – often referred to simply as Palmer's. If your ancestor lived or died in the London area during the 19th century, it is worth checking Palmer's, as *The Times* was very much a metropolitan paper. Indeed, the Ibrox Stadium disaster of 1908 in Glasgow – which saw over a hundred soccer fans killed – merited a mere paragraph, while cases before London magistrates were covered in detail.

You can use newspapers for all sorts of research. Local newspapers, for example, may include:

- Notices of births, marriages and deaths, and obituaries of prominent local people.
- Coverage of marriages and funerals – which may mention the names of people who were present and describe what the ceremony was like.
- Advertisements for or news items about local businesses or the sale of land – which may be of interest if, for example, your ancestor was a butcher or owned a pub.
- Accounts of the annual dinners of local societies or other organizations.
- Sports events – which may list the names of team members and prizewinners.

The UK's largest collection of newspapers is at:

The British Library Newspaper Library
Colindale Ave
London NW9 5HE
Tel: 020 7412 7353
Internet: www.bl.uk

'Old lady reading', 1902
(COPY 1/456)

Other reference books

Among other publications that may contain references to your ancestors – especially if they were well-to-do or famous – are the following, which can be consulted at the PRO Library:

- *The Dictionary of National Biography* – which has thousands of entries for famous (and not so famous) men and women. The entries are often very informative. A new edition is due to be published in 2004.
- *Who's Who* – which lists eminent (and, frankly, some less eminent) men and women of the day. When they die their entries are included in *Who was Who*, which is published every decade or so.
- *Burke's* and *Debrett's Peerage* – which give details about the nobility, including life peers, knights, baronets and some non-titled landed gentry. The Society of Genealogists has runs of these and rival publications.
- *The Dictionary of Labour Biography* – which offers biographies of activists in the labour movement.

There are also dictionaries of biography for many other professions.

- Reports of court cases – which are likely to mention the names of witnesses and defendants or litigants.
- News stories about accidents or deaths in suspicious circumstances. For instance, there might be a verbatim account of a coroner's inquest, or a report about a local person being killed by a train.
- During the two world wars, short obituaries of local people killed in action or in air raids, sometimes accompanied by photographs.

Further reading

Colin R. Chapman, *An Introduction to Using Newspapers and Periodicals* (FFHS, 1996)

Audrey Collins, *Using Colindale and Other Newspaper Repositories* (FFHS, 2000)

Directories

The most basic directories are simply published lists of names, usually arranged by address or by trade or profession. The first ones – usually lists of local gentry or traders – appeared in the mid 18th century, but directories really came into their own a hundred years later. The largest publisher of directories was the firm set up by Francis Kelly in 1845.

By the end of the 19th century there were:

- Street directories – listing the householder of every house in every street, sometimes with his or her occupation.
- Trade directories – listing local tradesmen and small businesses and the like, with their addresses.
- Court directories – listing the 'more respectable' middle and upper class members of the local community.

In addition, many professions produce directories of practitioners. The most famous of these is *Crockford's Clerical Directory*, published since 1858, which lists clergymen in the Church of England. Also widely known directories are the *Law List* and *Medical List*, for barristers and doctors respectively. Directories often

include short biographies of members and list promotions or honours awarded.

There is no national collection of directories, but both the Guildhall Library in London and the Society of Genealogists have large collections. Local studies libraries usually have directories for their area. The PRO Library has a small collection of street and trade directories. Many directories are now being copied and sold as microfiche or on CDs.

Lord Milner, 1903
(COPY 1/460)

Page from *Debrett's Peerage*, 1906, with entry for Lord Milner

You can use directories for:

- Checking the addresses of people – but bear in mind that the information in a directory may be a year or two out of date by the time of publication. As mentioned earlier, if you look at census records and a family are not at the expected address, it is worth checking to see whether they have moved round the corner.
- Checking occupations – in many working-class families the householder regularly changed jobs. You may therefore find that the entry in a trade directory differs from the one that appears in the census records.

Maps

Although the first maps date from the middle ages, map making as we know it really begins in the 18th century. Millions of maps survive – the Public Record Office alone has 5 million, both for the British Isles and other parts of the world, and most local studies libraries and record offices have maps for their own areas.

Five kinds of map are most likely to be of use:

Enclosure maps These were drawn up at the time when the land in a parish was 'enclosed' (divided up among the local landowners). This mostly happened between about 1750 and 1850. The maps show how the land was divided up. Incomplete sets are held at the PRO and local record offices.

Tithe maps These also relate to property ownership and were drawn up, under the Tithe Commutation Act 1836, to assess the amount of tax that was due to be paid to the Anglican church. The maps and the accompanying apportionments (assessments) show how much land an individual owned. Again, incomplete sets are held at the PRO and local record offices.

Valuation Office maps These maps are not very widely known – little wonder, as they are difficult to use. But persevere, because you will find that they are full of fascinating information about the houses your ances-

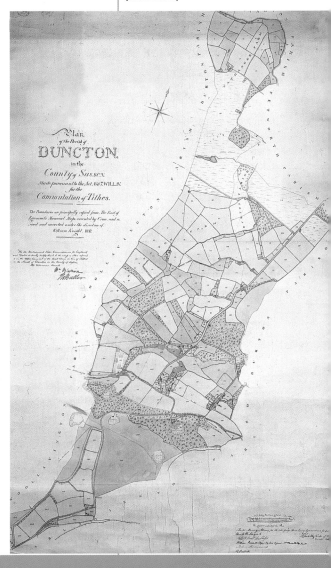

tors lived in just before the First World War. The maps and related field books, all of which are at the PRO, date from between 1911 and 1916. Drawn up as part of the valuation survey for a new land tax, they contain detailed descriptions of most properties in urban as well as rural areas.

Ordnance Survey maps Founded in 1791 to map the whole of the British Isles, the Ordnance Survey (OS) started to publish its famous inch-to-the-mile maps in the early years of the 19th century. By the middle of the century they had begun producing detailed surveys of towns, even down to indicating the location of lamp-posts. They will give you a good idea of the layout of an area. The PRO has a reasonable collection, as do many local archives. In addition, some bookshops and many libraries sell reproduction maps.

Census registration maps Between 1861 and 1921 the General Register Office pro-vided maps showing census enumeration boundaries. The set held by the PRO is incom-plete, but they can help iden-tify in which district London streets lay, as well as in which areas hamlets and isolated set-tlements can be found.

Tithe map of Duncton in Sussex, 1837 (IR 30/35/82)

Further reading
Nick Barratt, *Tracing the History of Your House* (PRO, 2001)
William Foot, *Maps for Family Historians* (PRO, 1996)

OTHER SOURCES

Many family historians come to the Public Record Office just to look at military records. Yet there are plenty of other records that contain information about our ancestors, and they are well worth exploring.

There is space to glance at only a few of these sources here. If you want to have a complete picture of the variety of resources that the PRO offers family historians, look at Amanda Bevan's *Tracing your Ancestors in the Public Record Office*, which gives an overview of everything from 18th-century acts for the relief of insolvent debtors to the births, marriages and deaths of British subjects in Zanzibar during the First World War. Truly, all human experience can be found at the PRO.

The sort of railway records you are likely to come across are:

- **Staff registers**

- **Pay records and registers**

- **Minutes – which often include notes about the appointment, promotion and dismissal of staff.**

- **Pension and benefit records**

- **Accidents – since all serious accidents were investigated in great detail.**

- **Staff magazines – which contain a lot about the movements and retirement of staff, as well as stories concerning such events as the award of a medal for a prizewinning allotment.**

Railway records

Although the railways were run privately until 1948, their records were taken over by British Railways at the time of nationalization and so are now largely to be found at the PRO.

From the outset, railway companies employed many hundreds of thousands of men and women. Even the smallest country station had a stationmaster, ticket clerks and porters. At the time of Queen Victoria's Diamond Jubilee, the London and North Western Railway claimed it had 70,000 employees. When the railways were nationalized in 1948, British Railways employed 641,00 people.

Wages were in general low and it was difficult to rise through promotion. It might take 20 years or so to become a train driver. There were compensations, such as sick benefits and pensions. Surprising numbers of women were also employed. Initially they ran station restaurants and bars and laundries, and worked in the offices. But during the two world wars women were taken on in large numbers to cope with the work previously done by men who had joined the forces.

The records are arranged by railway company. You therefore need to have a very good idea which company your ancestor worked for – as well as the type of work he (or she) did, as the records are sometimes broken down by occupation (signalman, driver, station-master, etc.). Often, if you know the station or depot where he worked that will help identify the company who employed him.

Each company kept records in its own way and there was little standardization. Also, the survival of records varies enormously. They are most complete for the Great Western Railway (GWR, or 'God's Wonderful Railway' to enthusiasts!), whereas little survives for many of the small companies that flourished in the mid-Victorian period.

Local archives may well have records about railways in their areas. Cheshire Record Office, for example, has an index and other records relating to people who worked at Crewe. The press is another useful source, as serious accidents would receive widespread coverage and local newspapers would report the retirement of prominent local officials. Records held by the National Railway Museum, in York, however, are largely about the technical side of railways.

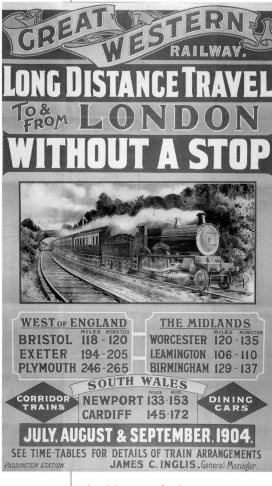

Advertising poster for the Great Western Railway, 1904 (COPY 1/218)

Further reading

Cliff Edwards, *Railway Records: A Guide to Sources* (PRO, 2001)

David Hawkings, *Railway Ancestors: A Guide to Staff Records* (Sutton, 1996)

Tom Richards, *Was Your Grandfather a Railwayman* (FFHS, 2002)

Immigration and emigration

The PRO has surprisingly few records about people who settled in Britain or left these shores to make new lives for themselves abroad. This is largely because the government was in general not very interested in these matters.

During the 19th century the British government prided itself on its liberal attitude towards resident foreigners – restrictions were first introduced during the first decade of the 20th century, with the aim of controlling Jewish migration from Russia and Poland. In Britain, unlike most other European countries, aliens did not have to register (except during the two worlds war), so a potentially major source of records does not exist.

At the same time, the government was keen to encourage emigration, particularly of the poor to British colonies – although it was less enthusiastic about organizing or paying for schemes. The millions of Irish men and women who found their way to America in the wake of the Great Famine in the 1840s did so largely under their own steam. The major exception to this was the transportation of thousands of petty criminals to Australia in the first half of the 19th century.

Immigration

It may already be clear that you have immigrants in your family tree, or it may be something you discover as you go about your research. Many people, for example, find that they have Huguenot ancestors – the French Protestant refugees who settled in Britain about 1700. A great deal of research into their history has been published by the Huguenot Society, and many of these publications can be consulted at the Society of Genealogists and at the PRO and FRC.

Most migrants to Britain were attracted by economic opportunities, perhaps as waiters or governesses, or just drifted here for one reason or another. The great writer Joseph Conrad, for example, arrived as a penniless Polish sailor. By the end of the 19th century most towns and cities had small close-knit

communities of Polish or Russian
Jews, Italians and Germans (although
the majority of the German community was to be expelled during and
after the First World War). Only the
East End of London and the dock-
land areas in other cities (especially
Liverpool, Cardiff and Glasgow) had
anything comparable to the melting-
pot of nationalities in America. By far
the largest community, however, was
the Irish – but as they were regarded
as British citizens there are no
records of their departure from Ireland, which was part of the United
Kingdom until 1921.

Foreigners should appear in the
census. Indeed great efforts were
made by the authorities to ensure
that they completed the forms –
although normally only their country
of birth and not the town or province
was included (and the same was
true for people born in Ireland and
Scotland).

Passenger lists begin in 1878, but
were only kept for ships that arrived
in Britain from outside Europe and
the Mediterranean. However, there are several earlier
series of records that may be relevant, such as the certificates of aliens arriving in UK between 1836 and
1852, which are arranged by port of arrival. Each certificate includes the individual's nationality, occupation and signature and notes the date of arrival and the
last country visited. There is an index of German
arrivals, but otherwise these records remain
unindexed. In addition, there are incomplete lists
of immigrants arriving from Europe between 1836
and 1869, drawn up by the master of the ship on
which they arrived.

Few people became naturalized, except by marriage, as it was an expensive process and conferred

Immigrants, from
George Sims'
Living London, 1901

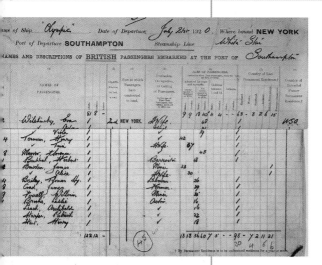

Passenger list for HMS *Olympic*, with entry for Archibald Leach (Cary Grant), 1920

few additional rights. Before 1844 to become a naturalized citizen required an act of Parliament. Most people chose the cheaper option of denization – becoming British subjects without the full rights of a citizen, which meant that they could not hold public office nor inherit land. There are records of denization and naturalization from the 15th century (from 1844–1922 they are to be found among Home Office records), and indexes up to 1961 can be seen in the Research Enquiries Room at Kew and at the FRC. Also, announcements and indexes for both naturalization and denization were published in the *London Gazette*.

Emigration

The best place to start is with the records of the country to which your ancestors emigrated – most often the United States or one of the colonies within the Empire – as these are likely to be much fuller. For example, passenger lists for ships arriving in the United States begin in 1819, whereas lists for ships leaving Britain don't start until 1890. There are numerous books and an increasing number of websites and CD-ROMs that can help you track down ancestors who sought a new life across the Atlantic or in Australasia. However, it wasn't uncommon for people to work for a few years in the United States then return to their family in Britain when they became homesick or had made their fortune – which often explains why somebody, particularly a young man, apparently disappears and then reappears years later. For example, W.H. Davies – author of *The Autobiography of a Super-Tramp* – embarked for America 'full of hope and expectation' only to return home some time in the 1870s after failing to make a go of it.

Passenger lists for ships bound for destinations out-side Europe and the Mediterranean begin in 1890 and finish in 1960. They list everybody in each party and include age, occupation and address in Britain. Because there are so many passenger returns, to stand a reasonable chance of success you need to know the port where your ancestors sailed from, the year and month, and the name of the ship.

There were very few government schemes to encourage emigration, although some records do exist. Perhaps the best known of these was the doomed plan by the New Zealand Company to recreate an ideal-ized British society in the untamed New Zealand bush – for which there are detailed records of the applicants, together with references and other notes. Another scheme was to encourage discharged soldiers to settle in the colonies, as the basis of a militia which could be deployed if there was trouble.

Further reading
Roger Kershaw and Mark Pearsall, *Immigrants and Aliens: a Guide to Sources on UK Immigration and Citizenship* (PRO, 2000)

Roger Kershaw, *Emigrants and Expats: a Guide to Sources on UK Emigration and Residence Overseas* (PRO, 2002)

Changes of name
There is no legal obligation to register a change of name – provided you don't attempt to deceive others, you can call yourself what you like. Indeed one of the pitfalls of genealogical research is that you may miss references to ancestors who were known by a nick-name or didn't use their given name, because they are likely to be referred to differently in formal docu-ments such as birth, marriage or death certificates.

However, there have always been people who wanted to formally change their name. A common reason in the 19th century was to comply with the terms of a will in order to inherit an estate, and during the First World War German and Jewish emigrants often adopted British surnames in order to avoid per-secution. The PRO has indexes of such changes, com-

Cary Grant

'Fishing in preserved waters', Trafalgar Square, 1892 (COPY 1/409)

monly known as deed polls, from 1851. In addition, intended name changes have been advertised in the government's official newspaper, the *London Gazette*, since 1914.

Police records

The records of police forces are normally held by either the police themselves or the local record office. The survival of material is patchy, particularly with regard to personnel records of individual officers. The PRO holds records of London's Metropolitan Police ('the Met') and the Royal Irish Constabulary.

The Metropolitan Police was under the supervision of the Home Secretary from its foundation in 1829 until responsibility passed to the new Mayor of London in 2000 – which is why their records are at the Public Record Office.

The PRO has service records for the Met from 1829 to 1933, although they are incomplete. Other less well known items among these records include registers of habitual criminals and drunkards for the period before the First World War.

The Royal Irish Constabulary was responsible for policing Ireland, except for Dublin, between 1836 and the establishment of the Irish Free State in 1921. The PRO has service records and some pension records for men who served in the force.

Merchant seamen

Family legend points to generations of Fowlers serving in the merchant marine, although I have been unable to find any trace of them in the various series of records about merchant seamen and officers at the PRO. But then few of my direct ancestors were who they claimed to be!

The earliest of these records date from the second half of the 18th century, in the form of ships' log books which list crew members. The survival of the records is somewhat patchy, however – seamen were registered between 1835 and 1857, then registration did not resume until 1913. The later records (which the PRO have on microfiche up to 1941) are particularly informative, with photographs, personal descriptions and details of ships served on. There are also numerous other short-lived series of records between 1835 and 1913 which may provide information. It certainly helps, before you start looking, to know your ancestor's rank and what he did – whether he was an engineer, deck hand, mate, etc.

Further reading
Kelvin Smith, Chris Watts and Michael Watts, *Records of Merchant Shipping and Seamen* (PRO, 1988)
Imperial War Museum, *Tracing Your Family Tree: Merchant Seamen* (IWM, 2000)

Apprentices
Until fairly recently the only way to learn a trade was to become an apprentice and serve an agreed period during which you learned from a master. Legal documents called indentures were signed, setting out the obligations of both the master and the apprentice, although for many employers, apprentices were little more than cheap labour.

The survival of such indentures is patchy. The Society of Genealogists has a reasonably large collection – and many can be found at local record offices, particularly among parish and Poor Law records, as many orphans and poor children were indentured to learn a trade. Livery companies in the City of London also arranged the apprenticeship of many children to trades, and these records are either at the Guildhall Library (see p. 78) or with the company itself. The Goldsmiths' Company has a particularly fine collection.

There is no national index of apprenticeships, but the tax records kept between 1710 and 1804 list the names and trades of masters and apprentices and the dates of indenture. These records (which are by no means complete, as there was much evasion and many exemptions were granted) are to be found at the PRO and there are copies of the index from 1710 to 1774 at both the PRO and the SoG.

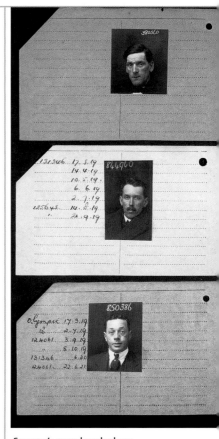

Seamen's record cards showing *Titanic* crew survivors Priest, Prior and Pugh (BT 350)

'The Shoemaker', 16th-century woodcut

Crime does pay!

At least there's a pay-off if you have criminal ancestors, because you can find a great deal of information about them in the records.

The records themselves are divided between the PRO and local record offices. Local archives have material from the magistrates courts and quarter sessions, which in general tried the less important cases, such as sheep stealing or fornication. The PRO has the records of the more major criminal courts, including the assize courts and the Central Criminal Court (the Old Bailey), and also of the Exchequer and Chancery courts which tried the more important civil cases. You will also find records about bankruptcy and debt at the PRO.

The quarter sessions records are a particularly interesting source – because, as well as records of trials, they include a great hotchpotch of material ranging from the returns of friendly societies and freemasons to licenses granted to publicans and gamekeepers. This is because until 1889 they had administrative responsibilities for a number of local services, including elements of the Poor Law. Magistrates, either alone or with colleagues, interrogated applicants for poor relief about their eligibility or endeavoured to discover the fathers of illegitimate children. The resulting reports of interviews and the accompanying paperwork can make fascinating reading. Unfortunately the survival of quarter sessions records is rather patchy, many counties having almost no records at all, but it is easy to cheat as catalogues are increasingly to be found on the internet at www.pro.gov.uk/a2a.

There are, however, two problems with criminal records. The first is that the documents themselves

Indictment of John Palmer, alias Dick Turpin, for stealing a mare (Black Bess), at Welton, Yorkshire, 1 March 1739 (ASSI 44/54)

Age (on discharge)	*11*
Height...................................	*4 ft 4 ½*
Hair.....................................	*Brown*
Eyes....................................	*Brown*
Complexion.............................	*Fresh*
Where born.............................	*Surrey*
Married or single	*Single*
Trade or occupation	*None*
Any other distinguishing mark	*Scar left*

Description when liberated.

side of neck

Photograph of Prisoner.

Thomas Savage,
Wandsworth Gaol, 1872–3
(PCOM 2/290)

were not, of course, designed with the family historian in mind and normally just record the processes in a trial together with the final judgement. And secondly they can be difficult to read. Indeed, often the clerk noted down the decision or process completed with a barely decipherable scribble (after all, he wasn't thinking of people looking through the material two or three hundred years later). Matters are further complicated by the fact that until 1733 a considerable proportion of legal records were written in Latin, and even after that date Latin phrases or abbreviations commonly crop up in the documents.

These records are not for the faint-hearted – but if you have any criminal ancestors in your family (as probably most of us do), their trials may provide a fascinating insight into their lives and the world they lived in.

Further reading

Michelle Cale, *Law and Society: An Introduction to Sources for Criminal and Legal History from 1800* (PRO, 1996)
Jeremy Gibson, *Quarter Session Records for Family Historians* (FFHS, 1995)
Ruth Paley, *Tracing Criminal Ancestors* (PRO, 2001)

KEY DATES

Historical events	Date	Genealogically important events
Battle of Hastings	1066	
	1086	Domesday Book
Henry VIII on throne	1509	
	1538	First parish registers
Elizabeth I on throne	1558	
	1563	Statute regulating employment of apprentices
Armada	1588	
	1598	Start of bishops' transcripts
Establishment of East India Company	1600	
	1601	Start of Old Poor Law
Charles I on throne	1625	
Commonwealth	1649–60	
	1650	Establishment of Quakers
The Restoration	1660	
Charles II on throne		
	1662	Law of Settlement
	1662–89	Hearth tax
	1665	Coldstream Guards (oldest regiment) formed
	1666	*London Gazette* first published
Establishment of Royal Hospital, Chelsea	1681	
James II on throne	1685	
	1687	Establishment of Bevis Marks (Britain's oldest synagogue) in London
	1689	Act of Toleration eases conditions for nonconformists
'Glorious revolution'		
William and Mary on throne	1689	
Anne on throne	1707	
	1710	Introduction of stamp tax on apprentices' indentures
George I on throne	1714	
George II on throne	1727	
	1731	Start of *Gentleman's Magazine*
	1733	Now all legal documents written in English
	1738	Establishment of Methodists
	1742/3	Start of register of births of nonconformists at Dr Williams's Library

Captions: Oliver Cromwell (SP 63/281)
Early railway illustration (COPY 1/31)
Queen Victoria's Diamond Jubilee ticket (COPY 1/134)
Poster for Festival of Britain 1951 (WORK 25/234)

Historical events	Date	Genealogically important events
	1749	First publication of *Navy List*
Change to Gregorian calendar	1752	
	1754	Earl of Hardwicke's Marriage Act regulates marriage in church
	1754	Start of regular publication of Army List
	1757	Reform of militia
George III on throne	1760	
	1760	Introduction of soldier's documents
	1761	Start of Regimental Registers noting births, marriages and deaths in the armed forces
American War of Independence	1776–83	
	1782–1853	Newgate Calendar lists prisoners tried at the Old Bailey
	1785	First issue of *The Times*
'First fleet' arrives in Australia	1788	
	1791	Catholic Relief Act legalizes Catholic churches and priests
	1791	Establishment of Ordnance Survey
French Revolution	1789	
French Revolutionary and Napoleonic Wars	1792–1815	
	1796	Start of death duties
	1801	First census
Battle of Trafalgar	1805	
	1812	Rose's Act regulates the way parish registers are kept
Battle of Waterloo	1815	
George IV on throne	1820	
	1829	Establishment of Metropolitan Police
William IV on throne	1830	
Liverpool & Manchester Railway opened	1830	
Great Reform Act	1832	
	1834	Start of New Poor Law
	1836	Tithe Commutation Act

Historical events	Date	Genealogically important events
Victoria on throne	1837	
	1837	1 July – Start of civil registration in England and Wales
Public Record Office established	1838	
First postage stamps	1840	
	1841	First census from which individual records survive
	1844	Liberalization of naturalization procedures
Great Famine in Ireland	1844–9	
Great Exhibition	1851	
	1851	Census
	1853	Royal Navy introduces continuous service engagement books
Crimean War	1854–6	
	1855	Introduction of civil registration in Scotland
	1856	First awards of Victoria Cross
Indian Mutiny	1857	
	1857	Introduction of civil divorce proceedings
	1858	Introduction of central probate system
	1858	First edition of *Crockford's Directory*
	1861	Census
	1864	Introduction of civil registration in Ireland
	1866	Age of the deceased shown in GRO death registers
Establishment of universal education	1870	
	1871	Census
	1871	Abolition of purchase of commissions by Army officers
	1875	Penalties introduced for failure to register births, marriages and deaths
	1881	Census
	1884	Married Women's Property Act allows wives to make wills
	1891	Census
Diamond Jubilee	1897	
Boer War	1899–1902	
Edward VII on throne	1901	
	1901	Census

Historical events	Date	Genealogically important events
George V on throne	1910	
	1911	Establishment of Society of Genealogists
	1911	Census
	1911	Mother's maiden name shown in GRO indexes
	1911–16	Valuation Office survey of property
	1912	Name of both spouses shown in GRO marriage indexes
First World War	1914–18	
Introduction of conscription	1916	
Establishment of Royal Air Force	1918	
Grant of vote to women	1918	
Division of Ireland into Irish Free State and Northern Ireland	1921	
General Strike	1936	
	1927	Introduction of adoption as a legal process
	1929	End of Poor Law
Edward VIII on throne	1936	
Abdication crisis	1936	
George VI on throne	1936	
	1939	Introduction of identity cards
Second World War	1939–45	
Battle of Britain	1940	
Introduction of Welfare State	1946	
Festival of Britain	1951	
Elizabeth II on throne	1952	
Suez invasion	1956	
	1961	Establishment of Institute of Heraldic and Genealogical Studies
Decimalization	1971	
	1974	Formation of Federation of Family History Societies
	1974	GRO indexes moved from Somerset House to St Catherine's House (and to the Family Records Centre in 1997)
	1977	PRO at Kew opened
	1997	Opening of Family Records Centre Public Record Office moves from Chancery Lane

FESTIVAL OF BRITAIN

1951

MAY 3 – SEPTEMBER 30

Key websites

Public Record Office
www.pro.gov.uk

The PRO's website offers an amazing resource for family historians. There are online versions of leaflets that explain the records simply, an index to all 9 million records held at Kew, and links to the 1901 census at www.census. pro.gov.uk and to other archive websites, including catalogues of material held by local record offices.

A related site is www.familyrecords.gov.uk, a portal site which includes links to the websites of UK national archives including the FRC.

Genealogy of the United Kingdom and Ireland
www.genuki.org.uk

This should be the first port of call for anybody with British and Irish ancestors. It has lots of resources and links to other sites.

FamilySearch
www.familysearch.org

The International Genealogical Index (IGI), which has long been an essential research tool, has now been largely replaced by the Family-Search website (see p. 31). This contains details of millions of people extracted from parish registers and other sources. Unfortunately it is not very accurate, so you should check any information you download against the original records.

Historical Manuscripts Commission
www.hmc.gov.uk

Through the National Register of Archives (see p. 20), the HMC maintains details of collections of material held by local record offices. The index is available online. The HMC site also includes links to other archive websites and 'focus' pages, which contain some useful advice for family historians.

Cyndi's list
www.cyndislist.com

Cyndi's List is the most wide-ranging family history website, with links to more than 100,000 websites around the world. Whatever your interest and wherever your ancestors came from, there is bound to be a website for you.

Other sites worth visiting
www.earl.org.uk/familia provides an overview of genealogical material held by local libraries. It is by no means complete or up-to-date.

www.englishorigins.com provides online access, for a fee, to an increasing number of databases held by the SoG.

www.ffhs.org.uk is the website of the Federation of Family History Societies. It provides a link to member societies plus a chance to buy genealogical books online.

www.rootsweb.com has hundreds of different resources available for the family historian. Although it is a mainly American site, there is some excellent British material, including the BMD project which aims to make the index to birth, marriage and death records available online.

Useful addresses

There are hundreds of archives in the British Isles – far too many to list here, but below are some of the places you may need to visit during the course of your researches.

England
National Register of Archives
Historical Manuscripts Commission
Quality House
Quality Court
Chancery Lane
London WC2A 1HP
Tel: 020 7242 1198
Internet: www.hmc.gov.uk

Guildhall Library
Aldermanbury
London EC2P 2EJ
Tel: 020 7606 3030
Internet: www.ihrinfo.ac.uk/gh/

Imperial War Museum
Lambeth Road
London SE1 6HZ
Tel: 020 7606 3030
Internet: www.iwm.org.uk

London Metropolitan Archives
40 Northampton Road
London EC1R 0HB
Tel: 020 7332 3820
Internet: ww.corpoflondon.gov.uk/lma

National Army Museum
Royal Hospital Road
London SW3 47DX
Tel: 020 7773 0717
Internet: www.national-army-museum.ac.uk

Maritime Research Centre
National Maritime Museum
Greenwich
London SE10 9NF
Tel: 020 8312 6691
Internet: www.port.nmm.ac.uk

Royal Air Force Museum
Grahame Park Way
London NW9 5LL
Tel: 020 8205 2266
Internet: www.rafmuseum.org.uk

Royal Naval Museum
HM Base (PP66)
Main RD
Portsmouth PO1 3HN
Tel: 023 9272 3795
Internet: www.rnm.org.uk

Society of Genealogists
14 Charterhouse Buildings
Goswell Road
London EC1M 7BA
Tel: 020 7251 8799
Internet: www.sog.org.uk

Wales
National Library of Wales
Aberystwyth
Dyfed SY23 3BU
Tel: 01970 623816
Internet: www.llgc.org.uk

Scotland
National Archives of Scotland
HM General Register House
Edinburgh EH1 3YY
Tel: 0131 535 1334
Internet: www.nas.gov.uk

The Scottish equivalent of the PRO. The NAS has documents such as nonconformist records and testaments (wills), which can be very useful.

General Register Office for Scotland
New Register House
3 West Register Street
Edinburgh EH1 3YT
Tel: 0131 334 0380
Internet: www.gro-scotland.gov.uk

The GRO(S) has Scottish birth, marriage and death certificates from 1855, census records, and Old Parish Registers from the 15th century.

Ireland
National Archives of Ireland
Bishop Street
Dublin 8
Tel: 003531 4072300
Internet: www.nationalarchives.ie

This is the Irish Republic's equivalent of the Public Record Office. It also holds pre-1922 material on Northern Ireland.

General Register Office
8–11 Lombard Street East
Dublin 2
Tel: 003531 6354000
Internet: www.groireland.ie

The GRO holds births, marriage and death records for Ireland between 1864 and 1921, and for the Republic from 1922 to the present day.

Public Record Office of Northern Ireland
66 Balmoral Avenue
Belfast BT9 6NY
Tel: 028 9025 5905
Internet: proni.nics.gov.uk

PRONI is Northern Ireland's most important archive. As well as official records, it has considerable holdings of personal and business papers going back before partition.

Useful publications

PRO Pocket Guides

(Pocket Guides offer concise introductions to selected genealogical topics.)

David Annal, *Getting Started in Family History* (PRO, revised edition 2001)
David Annal, *Using Birth, Marriage and Death Records* (PRO, revised edition 2001)
David Annal, *Using Census Returns* (PRO, revised edition 2001)
Simon Fowler, *Tracing Irish Records* (PRO, 2001)
Simon Fowler, *Tracing Scottish Records* (PRO, 2001)
Simon Fowler, *Using Poor Law Records* (PRO, 2001)
Michael Gandy, *Tracing Catholic Ancestors* (PRO, 2001)
Michael Gandy, *Tracing Nonconformist Ancestors* (PRO, 2001)
Karen Grannum, *Using Wills* (PRO, revised edition 2001)
Bruno Pappalardo, *Using Naval Records* (PRO, revised edition 2001)
William Spencer, *Using Army Records* (PRO, new edition 2001)

PRO Reader's Guides

(Reader's Guides look at aspects of the records in more detail.)

Amanda Bevan, *Tracing your Ancestors in the Public Record Office* (PRO, 6th edition 2002)
Stella Colwell, *The Family Records Centre* (PRO, 2002)
Jane Cox, *New to Kew?* (PRO, 1997)
Cliff Edwards, *Railway Records* (PRO, 2001)
Simon Fowler and William Spencer, *Army Records for Family Historians* (PRO, 1998)

Kelvin Smith et al., *Records of Merchant Shipping and Seamen* (PRO, 1998)
William Spencer, *Air Force Records for Family Historians* (PRO, 2000)
William Spencer, *Army Service Records of the First World War* (PRO, 3rd edition 2001)

Reference books and introductions to family history

Robert Blatchford, *The Family and Local History Handbook* (published annually by the Genealogical Services Directory)
Jeremy Gibson and Pamela Peskett, *Record Offices: How to Find Them* (FFHS, 1998)
Mark Herber, *Ancestral Trails: The Complete Guide to British Genealogy* (Sutton, 1999)
David Hey, *The Oxford Companion to Local and Family History* (Oxford University Press, 1996)
George Pelling, *Beginning your Family History* (FFHS, 1998)
Reader's Digest, *Explore your Family's Past* (Reader's Digest, 2000)
Pauline Saul, *The Family Historian's Enquire Within* (FFHS, 1995)
John Titford, *Succeeding in Family History: Helpful Hints and Time-saving Tips* (Countryside Books, 2001)

Family history magazines

There are several magazines for genealogists. The PRO publishes *Ancestors* six times a year; it can be bought at the PRO and FRC bookshops and is also is available by subscription. Many newsagents sell *Family History Monthly*, *Family Tree Magazine* and *Practical Family History*.